MW00715149

The Secret Admirer

and Other Stories

Study Guide with Leaders Notes

By Donald L. Deffner
Earl H. Gaulke, Editor

SAINT LOUIS

Editorial assistant: Pegi Minardi

To
a very patient woman
my wife, Corinne

CONTENTS

Helps for the Leader

ABOUT THIS BOOK

Everyone loves a story!

In India a native evangelist has a bicycle, a lantern, and a drum. He goes into a village, people gather at the sound of the drum, and he tells them a story. It is the story of Jesus.

Jesus Himself told stories.

> Jesus used parables to tell all these things to the crowds; he would not say a thing to them without using a parable. (Matthew 13:34 TEV)

He would say, "A certain man was going down from Jerusalem to Jericho, when robbers attacked him ..." (Luke 10:30). And a hearer mentally responded, *Yes, Rabbi, why I know just what you are talking about! Why, Uncle Daniel was attacked on that road just last week!*

Jesus followed the principle of going "from the known to the unknown." He started with the real world of his hearers and them moved on to the theological truth involved.

Stories, thus, can enliven adult Bible classes and home-discussion groups. Our involvement in the characters' lives can quicken and enrich our concern for the issue involved—pride, gossip, loneliness, witnessing, etc.—and assist us as Christians in grappling with the question (as Francis Schaeffer puts it) "How should we then live?"

The following stories are offered as an issue-oriented resource for adult Bible study and discussion groups.

There are now four courses available, each session based on one to three short stories, arranged topically according to thematic issues, with discussion questions referencing Bible texts designed to lead the learner to apply Scripture to his/her own life. These are for use with small home-discussion groups or in the Sunday morning or week-day church Bible class. Additionally, the study booklets can simply be used by individuals—for their own individual reading, meditation, and spiritual nourishment.

Because the story/stories for each session can be read in an average of 9 minutes (range, 5–13 minutes), the stories may be read at the time of meeting—either silently by each participant before discussion or orally by volunteer readers in the group. A third alternative is that the stories be read beforehand.

Also, the stories can be shared with people outside the church. Indeed, "tell me *your* story" can be a fruitful cata-lyst in reaching out to others as we first *actively listen* to *them*. My friend Christian Zimmermann, a Lutheran pas-tor and the flight engineer on TWA flight 847, which was hijacked some years ago, went through a lot of suffering during that hijack, but also dared to share his Christian faith with his hijackers. Christian would ask them: "What do you believe?" And they would tell him. "Then he would ask: Now, what do you think I believe as a Christian?" And they would tell him. And then he would correct their mis-understandings about the Christian faith—and share the Gospel with them.

Something else may also occur in such a dialog. As J. Russell Hale, author of *Who Are the Unchurched*, says,

> Your tone of voice, gestures, etc., are very important as you say, "I'd like to have you tell me your story about what you think of the church. Go back to your childhood." *And they really open up.*

> If you listen when they tell you their story, a point will come when they'll say, "Tell me your story." And you don't hand out tracts, but as the two stories converge there is the miracle of dialog, the point when *God's story* can come out ... And the "rumor of angels" impinges on their ordinary experiences.

In whatever setting you use this book, may the Holy Spirit attend your reading. And then, may you be moved to share with others *The Story*.

Besides the discussion questions for each session, here are key questions to consider throughout the course:

1. Is the story true to life? Give reasons for your answer.
2. What, if anything, does the story have to say to our Christian faith and life?
3. How does it reveal or point to our need? (Law)
4. How does it point to or suggest God's action for us in Christ? (Gospel)

SESSION 1
Morality

The Secret Admirer

"Come in!" Frieda Schlaegel heard Pastor Tom Attenborough's cheerful voice from inside his study. She opened the door and there he was, beckoning her to a chair.

Frieda sat down and crossed her legs, consciously letting her skirt slip up over her knees. She smiled at him, winsomely. And he smiled back. Her "Pastor Tom." Her magnificent obsession.

"Well, what can we do for you today, Frieda?" he began.

But Frieda's reverie remained unbroken. Although she immediately launched into trivia about the upcoming church women's banquet, Frieda's mind was on Pastor Tom—*her* Tom.

Her infatuation with him had begun slowly when she and husband, Phil, had first joined the church three years ago. Frieda and Phil were childless, and the experience of being in the new fellowship had radically changed Frieda's life. Especially when Tom preached, Frieda was mesmerized, and it seemed that his eyes were boring into only hers. When he shook her hand at the door she was just sure he gave her hand an extra squeeze. And when he made pastoral calls in her home, she was convinced he spoke to her more than Phil, and gave little clues with his eyes and hands as to how much he was drawn to her.

And so her infatuation had grown and increased until

11

she could almost burst. And finally, today, she had decided she would have to declare her love for him. She hadn't really thought it all through yet. But certainly Tom would understand. For, after all, there was the way he always looked at her, the hints he had given. "See you *later!*" he would say.

And so here she was, like a giddy school girl. Ready to let him know she responded to his affection. And then there would be this special understanding they would have, a "bonding," as it were.

Oh, she wouldn't want him to leave his wife and two small girls. It would be a discreet little affair. Something between just the two of them. Something her husband would never know about, either. Phil wouldn't guess a thing. He was always too busy at his hardware store anyway, day and night.

"Frieda!" She jumped, startled.

"The banquet speaker, Frieda, I asked you who the banquet speaker is three times. You seem to be a million miles away," he laughed.

"Oh, Pastor Tom," she responded, apologetically. "I'm so sorry! Pastor ..." She kneaded her handkerchief. A moment passed.

"Pastor ... *Tom* ... I'm really not here about the banquet. I'm ... I'm in *love* with you!"

She hesitated, breathing rapidly. "I can tell how you feel about me. And I felt that I should be honest with you and ... uh ..." She paused, and with a demure, almost modest tone added, "I wanted you to know ... *I return your affection.*"

A classic silence ensued.

Then, slowly, Frieda saw Pastor Tom leave his chair and stand beside her.

"You have no idea what it means to hear you say this, Frieda!" he began. And then he continued, quickly. He would leave his wife and girls, give up his parish. It *would* be "just the two of them," as the old song goes. He talked rapidly on and on about the plans they would make, the new life they would have. He wouldn't have any money, but ... He pulled her to her feet.

"I ... but ..." Frieda began, recoiling, her mouth and face

12

suddenly looking like a bug-eyed goldfish that had just swallowed a frog.

"That wasn't quite what I meant ..." she stammered, backing away.

Everything was going all wrong. She'd just wanted him to know how she felt ... a little affection on the side ... a little romance.

"No, no, *no!*" she cried. "I didn't mean that you would give up everything." She stumbled toward the door. "I didn't mean that—I just ..."

And then, quickly, it was over. He looked hurt, grieved. It was a great loss, he said, but he understood. They would keep this little conversation a secret between them. Although they would both *know*, they would never speak of it again, right? *Agreed!* He would try to get over it. Throw himself back into his work. And ... Oh, yes, she agreed, of course no one else would ever know. Oh, yes. *Total silence* about it. Good-bye. I'm sorry, Pastor.

Frieda stumbled out the door and across the parking lot toward her car. *That maniac! What was he thinking about? It wasn't what she had intended. He was going too far. I only wanted to ...*

Wide-eyed, she jumped into her car, started it, and screeched out of the parking lot.

Rev. Tom Attenborough drew back from the slit he'd been peering through in the venetian blinds and sat down at his desk. Well, that was the third one now in his parish. It was a risky approach, but so far it had worked.

He sighed, turned on his computer, and continued writing next Sunday's sermon.

For Discussion

1. Could an incident like this have really taken place?

2. Do you feel Frieda is responsible for her feelings, or was she "led on" by the pastor?

3. What do you feel really made Frieda pursue this course of action with the pastor?

4. If you were Frieda's friend, what would you say to her and how would you help her? (Consider 1 Corinthians 10:13.)

5. How do you evaluate the pastor's approach in responding to Frieda? Is he guilty of a "misuse of power"?

6. Satan takes particular pleasure in attacking the moral stability of pastors. In your experience, when pastors "fall," has it more often been their fault or that of their temptress? or tempter!?

7. What are the scriptural criteria for a pastor's moral life? See 1 Timothy 3:1–7; Titus 1:5–9.

8. Is it all right for a married person to "bond" with a person of the opposite sex if only for the purposes of a deep, enriching friendship?

9. How does one avoid "magnificent obsessions" like Frieda's? See Matthew 4:10–11; 1 Corinthians 10:12–13; Philippians 4:8.

No Thanks for the Memory

Bud and Yvonne Parker left their home in Seymour, Indiana, and headed for Fort Wayne. The occasion was the 25th anniversary of their graduation from Hamilton High, where they had first met.

That was in the sixties. They were now in their late forties. Three children. Bud ran a farm-implement store. And Yvonne was a substitute teacher.

As they headed north, Yvonne said with irritation, "I still really don't know if I want to go."

"But, honey," responded Bud, "think of all the old high school friends we'll meet—some we haven't seen in 25 years!"

"Yeah, I know," said Yvonne ruefully. And she put her head back, closed her eyes, and pretended to doze.

Bud said no more, and in several hours they had arrived in Fort Wayne and checked into a motel room. The festivities began with a social hour at 6 p.m. The setting was a country club overlooking a lake. There were many cries of welcome, jokes about balding, paunchy, middle-aged men, and other kidding remarks. Most of the men had rented tuxedos for the night. But some women had donned the same dress they had worn to the graduation prom 25 years before. That is, if they still had it, or could alter it.

The evening progressed merrily with a fine dinner, several brief "roasts," and then a video composed of old movie clips people had made during their high school years together.

Then came the dance. And the moment Yvonne had dreaded. She could see him across the dance floor as he made his way toward her and Bud.

Russ Walker.

Yvonne's heart sank, but she tried to keep calm and just clung to Bud as they moved around the floor.

"May I cut in?" Russ asked. Before Yvonne could utter a word, Bud graciously said, "Of course," and had disappeared. And here she was, in Russ's arms again, as she had been so many times before she'd met Bud.

The dance music suddenly ended and Russ said, "I could use some cool air. Let's step outside—Okay?"

Yvonne nodded, a little indecisively. But she followed him out to a small veranda overlooking the lake. Most couples had headed for the other side of the building, where drinks were being served, and so they were alone.

It was good to breathe fresh air again. The night was balmy going on muggy, for it had been a typical Fort Wayne May. Winter had dragged on and on, there was no spring, and then suddenly it was another hot summer.

Yvonne looked around. No other couples were in sight.

"I hate you," she suddenly blurted out. "No, I *revile* you."

"What? *What!*" exclaimed Russ, responding as if he had been slapped. "What in the *world* are you talking about?"

Yvonne walked to the edge of the veranda and sighed. "You know, the last year of high school. The night we spent together that time—on Halloween—our little 'one night stand'!"

"Oh, *that*," said Russ, still stunned. "But ..." he began.

"Or *don't* you remember? Were there so many *others*?" She paused, then added quickly, "Oh, I don't really mean I *hate* you. I hate *myself*. I hate both of us for what we did."

She paused, and looking far out over the lake, sighed. "It's been plaguing me all these years."

Russ was just beginning to collect his thoughts now and spoke defensively, "But that was so long ago."

"Does that make it irrelevant, Russ? That it was twenty-*five* or twenty-*six* or *forty*-six years ago? Look..." She became calmer now and almost pleadingly began her words—words which she had composed in her mind many times. "Look, Russ, I've needed to say this for a long, long time. I don't hate you. I didn't mean that. I hate what we *did*. I guess it was my fault as much as yours. When Bud came along, and then you met Marilyn, it was over for us. But the *memory* of what we did lingered on."

Yvonne took a deep breath and looked out at the lake again. She spoke very softly.

"I've asked God's forgiveness many times ... I believe I've gotten it ... I've tried to forgive you. I *guess* I have ..." Her voice trailed off. She cleared her throat. "I guess ... I guess ... I've still got to ask you to forgive *me*. I was to blame, too."

"But that was *so long ago* ... I'd almost forgotten ..." Russ stammered again.

"Look, Russ. I'm a Christian. I thought you were one, back then. But does the fact that Christ died for us 'a long time ago' make His death irrelevant today? Oh, I don't want to sound preachy, but ..."

"Look, Yvonne, I hold nothing against you. Of course I forgive you if you need to hear me say that. But it was as much my fault as it was—if it was—yours. Let's call it square ... forgiven ... past ... Okay?"

A sense of relief seemed to settle down over Yvonne. *So the air was finally cleared*. In fact, all of a sudden the air felt rather chilly.

"Let's move," said Russ. "Still friends?"

Yvonne nodded a grateful assent, and they moved back toward the dance floor, where they could see their spouses, Bud and Marilyn, approaching them. A few pleasant words were exchanged, and Bud whirled Yvonne away to dance to an oldie from the sixties.

It was 2 a.m. before everyone sang "Auld Lang Syne" and they left the country club. Yvonne had been inseparable from Bud through every dance and politely refused all comers.

"Hey, you were a real clinger tonight, Babe," said Bud, teasingly, as he headed the car toward their motel.

Yvonne edged over the seat nearer to him, and lightly put her hand around his arm.

He added, "You seemed a little uptight back there for a while. Anything happen? You okay now?"

And then it all came tumbling out, between little sobs ... her conversation with Russ, and its resolution.

Bud was silent for a moment.

But then he said softly, "I wondered some times about you and Russ. But I loved you so much, and, anyway, it was such a long time ..."

Yvonne stiffened, but then she heard Bud quickly add, "No. I don't mean that. Whatever happened before we met is not meaningless. But when I married you I accepted you as you were ... as God has accepted *me* ... you ... *us*. Because

18

of what He did for us ... 'a long time ago.' "

Yvonne looked wistfully at her husband.

"Bud," she said. "I started loving *you* 'a long time ago', too ... and I still do."

Bud flashed a quick grin at her and then looked straight ahead at the road ... a beautiful, long way ahead.

For Discussion

1. Need Yvonne have "confessed" to her husband? Would you have done so? Does one have to reveal everything from one's past to have a truly honest marital relationship?

2. If your mate had made a similar confession to you, how would you have reacted to it?

3. To avoid hypocrisy, how much should we share with our friends about our weaknesses and sins?

4. Aren't some sins practically "unforgivable"? If we can't avoid *remembering* a grave offense committed against us, how can we truly "forgive" it?

5. "Maybe God can 'forgive and forget' but humans can't."
   Do you agree? See Isaiah 43:25; Matthew 6:12, 14–15.

6. What is the nature of God's forgiveness? See Psalm
   103:11–12; Luke 23:34; Romans 3:23–26.

7. How often should one forgive? See Matthew 18:21–35;
   Colossians 3:13.

The Night Visitor

All day long he had heard them calling the man's name.
Harold this and Harold that. Harold! Harold! Harold! He
was growing sick of the name.

Ed lay in a hospital bed. He had been undergoing tests.
Everything had gone fine. His friends and children had visited him. And Mabel, his wife, had been faithfully at his
side. But now she was home with a cold. Today he had had
no visitors.

And so he had lain there, restless, listening through the
always open door to the conversations from the next room.

"I'm a practicing attorney," he could hear the man bray-
ing to the nurse. "I'm losing a lot of money lying in this
place." His voice was abrasive, arrogant. Ed detested the
man immediately.

Ed couldn't get out of bed by himself. He'd asked the
nurses to close the door as they left, but they'd forget. And so
he had lain there, forced to listen.

"Harold, the place isn't the same without you!" visitors

said. "Harold, you should see the new chick in the secretarial pool!" "Harold, you are quite a guy!" *Harold, Harold, Harold!*

Ed tried to watch TV, but it was consummately boring. Idiots talking to idiots on afternoon talk shows, confirming each others' permissive lifestyles and applauding like robots. The commercials particularly irked him. They were inevitably condescending, presuming the viewers were morons impressed by inane slapstick or promises of instant health and wealth. He pressed "mute" quickly when the commercials came on.

He *never* watched the soaps. Half the time a couple was in bed pawing each other, heaving and moaning. How could this stuff have ever gotten on TV without an *X* rating? Good thing kids were in school. The other half of the time the "actors" swaggered around fulfilling what they thought was the formula for success: "act arrogant and talk dirty." He'd never seen a soap actor yet who incarnated humility.

Ed tried the PBS channel. Occasionally an intelligent commentator came on. But he couldn't forget the smooth "modern" journalist talking about AIDS. Her daughter was 17 now, going off to college, and would be "establishing her sexual identity," the mother said brightly. She was concerned about her daughter's need for sexual freedom and yet feared she could get AIDS.

Ed reflected: Why didn't the mother just say the daughter was going to fornicate and sleep around now and had no self-control? He flicked off the set.

The day wore on. Harold's friends came and went—boisterous, raucous. They must think that room is the center of the universe.

Finally, evening. Some peace. Ed caught one good old flick on the TV, *Friendly Persuasion*, with Gary Cooper and Dorothy Maguire, and began drifting off to sleep.

A few hours later he was suddenly awakened by a sound in his room. What was it? In the darkness he saw a figure moving toward his bed. Then there was the faint smell of perfume. It was not Shalimar. That was Mabel's favorite.

The figure stood by his bed. Ed was fully awake now.

Maybe it was a nurse just checking on him. He'd pretend he was asleep.

Then he heard the rustle of starched clothing being slipped off and dropped to the floor. A woman's hand took his right arm, lifted it, and he felt her other arm shift the sheet on his bed as she lay down beside him.

Stunned, Ed could hardly realize what was happening, much less decide what to do. He stiffened.

"What's wrong?" a purring voice said. The aroma of the delicate perfume enveloped him.

"I can't," he whispered.

"But why not?" the voice said, teasingly.

A brilliant thought struck Ed.

"I ... I have a headache," he whispered huskily.

"But Harold, you promised me a C-note," the voice responded.

"I'm not Harold," Ed replied.

The woman gasped and wheeled out of the bed. Ed could hear her fall on the floor. Then he heard the rustle of her clothes as she quickly pulled them on and fled from the room.

Ed smiled.

And he wondered how Harold felt.

Waiting. Waiting. Waiting.

Ed smiled more broadly.

For Discussion

1. What would you have done if you had been in Ed's situation?

2. How do you evaluate Ed's feelings about Harold? Were they justified? How do you react to Ed's response at the end of the story?

3. Do you share Ed's feelings about television programs? Where do you think he is coming from theologically?

4. What is the *source* of temptation? See 1 Peter 5:8; Matthew 15:19; James 1:14–15; 1 John 2:15–16.

5. What is one of the easiest ways we can fall into temptation? See 1 Corinthians 10:12; 1 Peter 5:9.

6. What promises does God make to us in overcoming temptation? See 1 Corinthians 10:13; James 4:2b; Deuteronomy 33:25b, 27; Isaiah 41:10.

7. What is the best way to prepare oneself *before* a particular temptation comes? See 1 Peter 2:2; Romans 6:1–6; 1 Corinthians 11:26–28; Philippians 4:8–9.

SESSION 2
Trust

Just the Two of Us

I guess you could say Bill and Trish Hazelton had just about everything. Their suburban country home, a little ranch, really, was nestled in the hills above Happy Valley Road near Orinda, California. It was a secluded spot and yet they were only one-half hour away from San Francisco.

It was an idyllic life. Bill had a lucrative investment job in The City. And Trish, whose parents had left her a private income, owned a string of horses which they kept on their land adjoining their ranch. Now in their early thirties, Bill and Trish presented an attractive duo when they appeared at the Orinda Country Club. Bill was darkly handsome, six feet two inches tall, a smart dresser, and a terror on the tennis court. But in conversation he was reserved and meditative.

Trish, on the other hand, was a striking blonde. She still kept her elbow-length golden hair. And her azure eyes sparkled as she talked to you. She had, as her cocktail circle friends jealously but admiringly admitted, *panache*. Trish was dashing to the extreme. She had an elegance of manner, combined with a carefree, spirited self-confidence unequaled in her set. Outgoing and warm in conversation, she would sometimes embrace an almost total stranger after just a few moments of conversation. Men encircled her like bees do a hive of honey.

But Trish was absolutely faithful to Bill. Theirs was a good marriage, a genuinely intimate marriage. I guess you could say it was almost the perfect match. Except for one thing. Trish couldn't get pregnant.

Bill and Trish talked long and earnestly about what she could do to conceive a child. They took repeated tests from specialists in The City, and counseled with couples in the same situation. They heard about one couple in Walnut Creek who had adopted two children over a 10-year period and suddenly one day the woman herself was pregnant. Something had been "released" in her, and now she had her own child. Trish had heard this had even happened to women who worked closely with children, who held them and cared for them.

And so she decided she'd get into a setting where she could be near children. She resolved to cut back on the time she spent with her cherished horses, and on her long early-morning rides on the golden hills above Orinda. And she went back to school again, to do graduate work at St. Mary's College in nearby Moraga.

Ensconced in another golden valley, the quiet St. Mary's campus became an ideal sanctuary for Trish's rekindled hopes for fulfillment. The Spanish style buildings gave one the feeling you were in a toney Arizona resort. And the hushed, darkened chapel provided a new haven for Trish's repeated prayers to God for the gift of a child.

The courses were fascinating. She was surprised that she was not the oldest person in each class. Many of the women, and a few men, were into their forties, pursuing a second career. And her contacts with children, young and small, increased as she got her fieldwork experience in nursery schools, preschools, and in meeting the offspring of her classmates.

The weeks quickly slipped by as Trish's new life replaced her former one. Her horses also got still less of her attention as she worked late at night or early in the morning on papers due for class. Thank God their handyman Everette could keep the ranch going while they weren't around. For Bill also was gone more and more. He was heavily in demand out of town as a financial consultant and guest speaker, and spent many weekends in Chicago or New York City.

And with that distancing came a gradual distance in their marriage. At first there was no loss of spoken affection, but every separation made each reunion seem more and more like meeting a stranger for the first time. Eventually conversation became increasingly strained. And as the weeks went by, although they shared the same bed, two hearts more often beat as two. No hand reached out to touch the other. And for each the sound of silence replaced the former "Sleep well, honey."

One day Bill came home from work early. He didn't expect Trish to be back yet from classes. But he was surprised to see Everette waiting for him in his pickup truck.

"Evening, Mr. Hazelton, I couldn't reach you at work, sir."

"What is it, Everette?" asked Bill worriedly.

"It's Pasha, Miz Trish's favorite horse, sir. He's mighty sick. I've called the vet and he's at the barn. But it doesn't look good, sir. Not sure yet what it is. But Miz Trish would want to know, sir."

"Of course. Thanks, Everette. I'll try to get ahold of her as fast as I can."

Bill agitatedly tried every phone number Trish had given him to reach her at St. Mary's campus, but to no avail. Finally, in desperation, he jumped into his Porsche and sped out of the driveway for Moraga. In 15 minutes he was turning in to the picturesque campus. Screeching into a visitors parking space, he headed towards the building where Trish said most of her classes were held.

And there he saw her. She was beneath a huge eucalyptus tree. But she was not alone. Standing in front of her was a ruggedly handsome young man in his late twenties. Unobserved by them, Bill watched from a distance, his eyes narrowing, as their conversation became more and more intense and animated. Then the young man stopped speaking, and Bill could see Trish almost explode with emotion. Suddenly she kissed the young man on the cheek, gave him a quick hug, and shouting words he could not hear, she ran off towards a distant parking lot.

Bill was stunned. A bilious mixture of emotions began

to boil up inside him. He was crushed, resentful, and jealous all at once. A wave of self-pity engulfed him. Then anger took over.

Here she hadn't slept with her own husband for three weeks and now she's throwing her arms around another guy! Something had to be going on!

Enraged, Bill decided not even to try to find Trish in the other parking lot. He hopped into his Porsche, and sped home alone. He arrived at the ranch before Trish, poured himself a straight double Scotch, and plopped himself in a chair in the living room facing the front door.

Trish sailed through the door only moments later, her face radiant. Her joyous smile disappeared immediately when she saw Bill's dark, angry eyes.

"Who is he, anyway?" he asked acidly.

"Who ... *what?*" Trish stumbled into a chair, and, stunned, collapsed into it. She just stared at him, open-mouthed, with tears welling up in her eyes.

"The guy under the tree—your schoolboy lover?"

"You were *there?*"

"I *saw* you. The *two* of you!"

Trish sank back wearily into the chair and looked heavenward. A long painful sigh came from deep down within her.

She said nothing. Bill said nothing.

Then, finally, like after a moment of silent reflection at a funeral, Trish spoke. Her words now were tight, choked little utterances, barely audible—whispers. She was shattered.

"He's in a class on campus. This is the first time I've ever talked to him." Trish looked Bill squarely in the eyes, then out the window at the golden hills.

Bill tensed. His heart sank slowly, and fear started reaching up inside his throat like a clutching hand.

Painfully, Trish continued.

"This ... *person* ... is premed. He works part-time at a doctor's office—my doctor. My doctor was heading off on a three-day back-pack trip in the Sierras. He couldn't get me on the phone, and wouldn't be able to reach me for some time, but ...."

Trish paused again, and let out a weary sigh. The exuberance Bill had seen in her on the campus was totally gone now. Absolute defeat marked her face.

Trish arose and walked to the window. Again she looked out at the hills, her back to Bill.

"My doctor wanted me to know ...." She choked a little sob down. "He sent me the news through this assistant of his ... I'm finally pregnant. You're the father. And you don't *trust* me."

Bill looked at the floor, ashen-faced. He could think of nothing to say.

The Fatal Phone Call

Everyone in the congregation liked Pastor Dan Davidson. The women actually admired him, though he wasn't what you'd call a "ladies' man." But he was outgoing, affable. He was 42 and handsome. About six-foot-three, with neatly brushed hair and an easy smile with perfect white teeth.

A plain woman of 40, his wife Anna had never resented the attention women paid her husband. As a tightly knit family of four they spent a great deal of time together. But now the girls were away at college. And Anna was alone more often.

There were three couples in the parish who were especially close to them. Harold and Betty Jameson, Dick and Ruth Goldschmidt, and Bill and Tanya Evans.

Especially Bill and Tanya. They'd gone out to dinner with them more often than with others. And lately they'd sensed more of the tension growing between Bill and Tanya.

In their mid-30s, Bill and Tanya had never been able to have children. They'd tried everything. And from what Anna heard it seems Bill's body chemistry was the problem.

Pastor Dan had tried to calm Tanya's frustration. She sought his counsel one bright May day. Anna saw Tanya enter Dan's office the third time that week.

At the office Tanya confessed, "I feel so empty, Pastor Dan."

"Just Dan," he interrupted, flashing his broad smile.

"Okay, Dan. But I believe we've got it going now. I've had what I think is morning sickness and ... oh God, I hope I've finally conceived. I'm 35 and it's not too late. Bill and I have tried *so* hard, and he'll be *so* pleased we're finally going to have a child.

"I'm visiting the doctor this afternoon," she continued, "for test results. I'll call you later."

"Okay, Tanya," said Dan. "All the best!"

Dan made hospital calls all afternoon. When he stepped quietly into the kitchen from the garage at 5 p.m., he heard the phone ringing.

Alone upstairs, Anna also heard the phone. Picking it up she recognized Tanya's voice.

"I just wanted you to know, Dan, I'm not pregnant."

Anna replaced the receiver and stared at the coffee spots on the carpet by her side of the bed.

Slowly she rose, went to the closet and took down the suitcase she customarily used when she visited her mother.

Then she opened the other closet and got out her larger suitcase also.

For Discussion

Now let's focus on the thought processes of the characters involved in these stories.

What really motivated them to think the way they did? Are those thoughts ever your thoughts?

1. Who do you think was *initially* responsible for the strain in Bill and Trish's marriage? Do you think that is a fair question?

2. When a couple's careers diverge, what are the warning signs indicating estrangement? Similarly, for married or single persons, what causes friendships to falter or break up?

3. What *really* causes "the fire to go out" in the bedroom? (Consider Ephesians 4:26.)

4. In Trish's mind, what was the significance of the quick kiss and hug she gave the doctor's medical assistant?

5. Do you believe Bill was justified in his initial reaction to what he saw under the eucalyptus tree?

6. What do you think of the following statement?

I don't believe jealousy is all that bad. The dictionary says it means "(1) suspicious; apprehensive of rivalry; as, her husband was *jealous* of the other man." It also means "protecting" or "watchful." What's wrong with that? I don't want to lose my wife to someone else.

In fact, the other day, when I made a comment about my wife flirting with a guy, she said to me proudly, "Why, Frank! You're JEALOUS!" It made her feel good I was JEALOUS. And then she added teasingly, "I didn't know you CARED for me that much!"

7. In one sense, these two stories have a common theme. Of course, many other factors than inability to have a child threaten a marriage. The real issue at stake is *trust*. In a lecture, British evangelist Canon Bryan Green once spoke of how he first asked his wife to marry him. He asked her if she loved him. She responded negatively. Then he asked her if she *trusted* him. She replied affirmatively. "That'll be enough to get on with it!" he concluded happily. What does Scripture say about the right kind of (trusting) thoughts? See Romans 12:3; Philippians 4:8; Ephesians 4:31–32.

8. What is the first thing you look for as a man, as a woman, in a spouse? How do you prioritize the qualities you desire in a mate?

9. Whether you are single or married, what do you look for most in making a friend? See Proverbs 17:17a; Ecclesiastes 4:9–10; John 15:13.

SESSION 3
Pride

The Best Sunday School Teacher in the Congregation

Joe Harris froze. He had just overheard two boys in his high school Bible class discussing him behind the lockers in the church gymnasium.

"Mr. Harris? Oh, he thinks he's so cool," Tommy Davis told Jimmy Thompson. "He thinks he's the best teacher in the whole world. He's always patting himself on the back. But, man, *he ... is ... proud*. And he brags about himself.

"Oh, he wouldn't admit it. And yet he *talks* to us about *modesty* all the time. Being *humble* Christians. But is *he*? Not on your life, Buster!"

Joe stood stunned, perplexed. He must confront Tommy. But before Jimmy had a chance to respond to Tommy's comments, or Joe to intervene, a chorus of voices invaded the far end of the locker room. Quickly Joe exited the gym to join his family for the late service.

Joe didn't hear much of Pastor Bauer's sermon that day. He just stared straight ahead. And even Janelle, his wife, who usually looked at everyone in the pews, noticed something was wrong. He shrugged off her puzzled inquiry quickly.

And then he thought—and thought—and thought.

"*Me*? Proud? Bragging? Condescending to the boys? Well, who isn't proud? Who doesn't brag a little?" The thoughts tumbled in his mind.

When the choir rose to sing he saw him in the choir and thought, *George Davis!*

Now *there* is a man who fits Tom's description! George Davis, the other high school boys' Sunday school teacher at Trinity Church, epitomized everything Joe did not stand for. Davis thought he had it all. Or at least it seemed that way to Joe.

Maybe it was Davis's unpretentiousness that bugged him. Davis was a quiet guy, quite unlike Joe. He spoke little, and never pushed himself on people. He didn't have Joe's outgoing nature. But underneath he must be a very proud, self-confident person. Joe was sure of it.

And his teaching! He'd listened outside George's classroom once. Oh, George did know the lesson all right. But he didn't have the raucous stories that Joe always told. He just had a soft-spoken, unassuming manner in the way he related to the young people.

That bothered Joe. Davis must be so SURE of himself. So FULL of himself! Yes! That was it! HE'S the proud one! He's so DIFFERENT from me!

Janelle nudged Joe. He had stood up for a hymn and forgotten to sit down. Why did they stand sometimes and sit other times? he grumbled to himself.

Gradually, anger began to build in him. Me—proud? Oh, I can remember the times I've tried to reach out to George and he just sucked on his pipe and said little— maybe so *I* could make a fool of myself.

Joe couldn't wait for the service to end. As soon as the benediction was pronounced he told Janelle, "I'll meet you in the parking lot in 15 minutes ... I have to see one of my students." And he rushed off.

"Returning to the scene of the crime," he cynically laughed to himself. I'll tell Tommy and Jimmy a thing or two. I know they usually pick up stuff in their lockers before heading home.

And sure enough, as if the devil planned it himself, the boys were there again. Joe waited until several other boys left the locker room. Happily for him, Jimmy and Tommy remained. He listened, waiting for his opportunity to talk to them.

This time Jimmy spoke. "You know, Tommy, remember what you said before church about Mr. Harris? I've been thinking, he tries hard and wants to be a good teacher. But, you know ..." He paused, reflectively. "I guess the difference is that Mr. Harris wants to be a good *teacher*, but Mr. Davis really *cares* for us.

"Remember how he drops by our homes? He comes to our Little League games? He doesn't have to. He phones us when we're sick. I think he really *cares*. I don't know if Mr. Harris does."

"I guess ... yeah," Tommy responded. "Mr. Harris is our *teacher*. Mr. Davis is our *friend*."

This time Bill Harris didn't consider a "confrontation" with the boys. He just wanted *out*.

Outside, in the parking lot, it had started raining. Janelle was talking to Marjorie Ottemoeller, in the distance. Meanwhile the special-education bus from the nearby children's home pulled out of the parking lot.

He always liked to wave to the children. Running, he got near the bus just as it started off.

By now he was soaking wet. Little Jennifer Warner, four years old, saw him approach. Holding out her pint-sized umbrella, she said, "Here, teacher. Can I help you?"

"Of course! Hi, Jenny," he said. He knelt his 6'2", 227-pound frame under her little umbrella as the bus drove off and together they waved good-bye at the kids.

Suddenly, his knees and back aching, Joe Harris thought this was a pretty good prayer position.

"Except one become as a little child ..." "Humble yourselves ..." "Out of the mouths of babes ..." "A little child shall lead them ..."

I need to work on being this size, he thought to himself.

He hugged Jennifer and gave her a rainy kiss.

"I like you," she said.

"And I like you too, Jenny."

To himself he added, "And thank You, God. I guess I got my 'sermon' in the locker room today."

Then, with the rain pouring over the little girl and the

big man bent under the tiny umbrella, Joe Harris prayed:

"I'm sorry, Lord. I'm not a very good teacher, but I want to be. Help me also to be a loving and authentic *friend* to my students. Teach me how, Lord!"

Just a Servant

Mary Lou Patterson could just sense the adrenaline surging through her as she neared the end of her lecture.

"And that, my friends, is what it feels like to walk 'In the Footsteps of Jesus'!" With a triumphant little jerk of her head, she stepped back from the podium and sat down. Waves of applause wafted towards her. After enjoying the adulation for a long moment, Mary Lou rose and, affecting an air of gracious humility, bowed to the crowd. Another wave of applause washed over her, and, acknowledging the clapping once more, she walked, head high, off the stage.

Mary Lou was in the convocation center at Concordia University in Irvine, California. As president of the Orange County Bible League, she had just delivered her well-known lecture "In the Footsteps of Jesus," an account of her numerous visits to Israel. A small group of women soon surrounded her backstage, and it was a half-hour before the auditorium had fully cleared and she was free to leave the building.

She walked across the large flower-bedecked patio and headed up the hill toward her car. Mary Lou Patterson, 55, was immaculately dressed in a deep blue suit. Only a delicate gold necklace adorned her neck; a wrinkle or two graced her face; her hair showed just the slightest touch of gray. And she carried herself erect. After all, she was well known. She was the *president* of the Orange County Bible League.

Pausing in front of the administration building, Mary Lou surveyed the scene. Concordia University was an incredibly picturesque campus. Its Spanish-modern buildings were on the crest of a hill overlooking a whole sea of expensive, red-tile-roofed homes in Irvine, which stretched north several miles to John Wayne Airport. In the distance she could see planes landing slowly from the East. To the left, on the brink of the hill, was a small chapel. From there you could look out toward the Pacific Ocean, only 20 minutes away by car. What a setting! Orange County! And I *live* here, a native Californian, she thought proudly.

Mary Lou glanced at her watch. Nearly 3 p.m. She needed to grab some lunch. She never ate before she gave a talk. "Want my blood in my head, not in my stomach," she cleverly said to her friends.

It was a cool day. I could use the exercise, she mused. So she left her lecture notes in her Cadillac in the parking lot and started walking down the hill to a nearby restaurant. A roadrunner briskly whisked past her on its way up the hill. Overhead, in the bright, blue sky, huge Marine helicopters thumped their way toward nearby Santa Ana Marine Corps Air Base.

Mary Lou soon reached University Drive and, passing a huge field of ripening strawberries, crossed the street into a cluster of shops near the I–405 freeway. San Diego was only 90 minutes to the south. She'd be lecturing there next Tuesday. Mary Lou saw the restaurant sign, "HUDSON'S GRILL," and walked in. She'd heard the food was excellent. She proudly walked through the door—and saw that the restaurant was practically empty.

Well, that was understandable. It was mid-afternoon. She sat down at a table. The usual bevy of golden-haired, suntanned, shorts-clad waitresses was not in sight. Only one waitress saw Mary Lou come in, and she quickly walked toward her with a smile. She was plain, Mary Lou thought, about 40, typical working-class type. Mary Lou sniffed slightly as the waitress approached her.

"Good afternoon, ma'am!" she said brightly. "May I get you a menu?"

Mary Lou flicked an imaginary piece of lint off her sleeve. "No. I'd just like a caesar salad and some iced tea."

"Comin' right up!" The waitress smiled again and sailed off to the kitchen.

Mary Lou took a deep breath. Overly cheerful people annoyed her—and none more so than waitresses who got too friendly and didn't "know their place." It especially irked her when they'd say, "Hi! I'm Mary. I'll be your waitress tonight." Some day Mary Lou was going to say, "Hello. I'm Mrs. Mary Lou Patterson. I'm your customer. And you're here to serve me."

She put on her reading glasses and looked down her nose at a card on the table listing special desserts. Mary Lou thought back to her lecture again. She had been in top form. How the people had admired her! Well, she *was* an expert on the Holy Land. God had given her such gifts and insights! She reminisced momentarily on her successful, recent lecture tour and her last trip to Israel. People really should appreciate more for whom and what she was.

She saw the waitress approaching with her salad, and then noticed that the woman was wearing a small silver cross. An idea came into Mary Lou's mind.

"I see your're wearing a cross, my dear," she said sweetly.

"Oh, yes, I'm a Christian," the waitress replied. "Your salad, ma'am. I hope you enjoy it." She paused a moment. "It's slow here today ..."

Mary Lou sensed an opening and said with dignity, "I am a Christian, too. In fact, I'm the president of the Orange County Bible League."

"You *are*?" said the waitress, genuinely impressed.

Mary Lou could tell she was interested and, clearing her throat, added, "Yes, I've just delivered a lecture on 'In the Footsteps of Jesus.' I've been to the Holy Land many times."

The waitress's eyes widened, and, in fascination, she almost sat down, but then she checked herself and stood staring at Mary Lou.

Mary Lou delicately took one forkful of her salad and felt "on stage" again.

"Yes, my dear, it's fascinating to walk in the very places our Lord walked." She began to paint a series of scenarios and warmed to the occasion as she watched the waitress hanging on every word.

"And Jacob's well ..." She began another description.

"It *is* chilly and eerie down there, isn't it—so steep down those stairs to the well," added the waitress.

Mary Lou shot a puzzled look at her and continued.

"... and then from the bus you see these fields just filled with rocks and stones."

"It makes the parable of the sower really come alive, doesn't it?" said the waitress brightly.

A little irritated, Mary Lou went on, "But of course in all the Holy Land, to walk the *Via Dolorosa*, the Way of Sorrows, is the—"

"You can almost feel the weight of the cross on His shoulders as you walk up those twisting, narrow streets, can't you?" added the waitress.

Mary Lou was now definitely aggravated, and her mood darkened further as the waitress, with all due reverence and enthusiasm, continued to add her own detailed comments to Mary Lou's descriptions of holy sites around Jerusalem and Bethlehem.

Finally, in desperation, Mary Lou resignedly stopped her tour de force. In mock defeat she looked over her glasses at the waitress and said acidly, "Well, I guess you've seen more of the Holy Land than I have."

"Oh, no, ma'am," said the waitress with astonishment. "I've never been there. I've just read about it. But it's my life's dream to go to the Holy Land. How blessed you are to be able to go—and so many times."

Mary Lou threw her head back. Abashed, she listened as the woman quietly continued.

"My life's dream," she repeated, "if I could ever manage to do it, is to see with my own eyes where our Savior was. . ." She paused, then caught herself.

"But I shouldn't be boring you with my talk, ma'am. I'm just a waitress—just a servant. I enjoy serving people. I could never afford a college education. I have no money. My husband works up the hill at Concordia University as a gardener."

Catching a quick look at the kitchen, she added, "Thanks for visiting our restaurant, ma'am. God ... go with you."

And she walked away.

Mary Lou slumped in her chair, suddenly feeling as wilted as the picked-over salad in front of her. The simple reverence and downright humility of the waitress had left her dumbfounded. *She*—the president of the Orange County

Bible League. The world traveler. The expert on the Holy Land. Deep inside herself, Mary Lou suddenly felt that this woman had walked in Jesus' footsteps far more than she ever had.

"I'm just a servant," she had said. Mary Lou had certainly always considered herself as far more than a servant.

She cast her eyes down on the table and slowly wrapped her fingers around her glass of iced tea. She twisted the glass in circles, stopped, and then wiped off the moisture that the glass had left on the table. She breathed a prayer.

"Speak, Lord, for Thy servant heareth."

For Discussion

1. In "The Best Sunday School Teacher" why do you think Bill resented George Davis so strongly? One factor in his animosity and hostility was Davis's being "different" in his personality. Why do we have such a hard time accepting people who are different than we are?

2. What does Scripture have to say about the "difference of gifts"? What are its implications for our life together in a congregation? See 1 Corinthians 12; Romans 12:3–21; 1 John 3:14–20.

3. What did the boys mean by Mr. Davis being their *friend* as well as their teacher? Are there times this "friend" relationship can get in the way of good teaching?

4. A daughter added a note to her dad on a Father's Day card: "Thanks for talking *with* me ... always." What do you think she meant?

5. In "Just a Servant" Mary Lou took "pride" in her work and enjoyed lecturing. Is there anything wrong with that kind of pride?

6. What were the "cracks in the armor" of Mary Lou? Where did she "fall short"?

7. What qualities did you see in the waitress?

8. What does Scripture say about servanthood? See Matthew 20:26–28; Luke 22:27; John 13:14; Philippians 2:7.

9. What are the beginnings of pride in each one of us? How do we recognize it? See Luke 18:11; 1 Peter 5:5b–6; Revelation 3:17.

10. What are other ways in which pride asserts itself in our daily lives—in the church? at work? at home?

SESSION 4
Parenting

The Longest Walk
He Ever Took

So this is heaven! Norm couldn't absorb it all at once. And yet there was his beloved Sandra standing in front of him. Sandra—who had died 10 years before. He couldn't believe his eyes.

"Norm!" she said lovingly, and she embraced him.

"But how ..."

"You were on your way home from visiting Ruth and had an accident. You hit a telephone pole just one block from our house."

"But ..." Norm just couldn't drink it all in. It had happened so fast. In the twinkling of an eye ..."

"And you remember Maria, Norm."

Norm blinked and saw Maria standing there. Maria, the Mexican factory girl, Ruth's close friend.

"Hello, Mr. Anderson," said Maria. "You know," she said, smiling, "I am only here because of your daughter, Ruth."

And then Norm began to remember ...

(Now we all know that there is no memory in heaven of sad things that happened on earth. Being in the glorious, joy-filled presence of God blots out everything that has gone before. "All things are made new ..." There is "no more death,

41

no more grief, crying, or pain. The old things have disappeared ..." But for the purposes of our story ...)

Norm and Sandra had lived all their lives in the quaint little town of Cedarburg, Wisconsin, about 20 miles north of Milwaukee. It was a wonderful life. Norm's work at the bank was just eight blocks from their old rustic home on a quiet, tree-lined street. Their church was only four blocks away. Lake Michigan was minutes away. And there they spent many a carefree Saturday on Norm's boat in the early years of their marriage.

What more could a man ask? Cedarburg represented the best of all the old values. Good friends. "Salt of the earth," Norm always used to say. Cedarburg. *Home.*

And it was there that Ruth was born and raised. But tragedy had struck one day when Ruth was 10 years old. Returning alone from a shopping trip to Milwaukee, Sandra's car had skidded on an icy bridge, plunged into the river, and Sandra had drowned.

Norm was devastated, but he still had Ruth. His beautiful, beloved Ruth. Norm bravely carried on raising her the way Sandra would have wanted. And after high school Ruth went to Concordia University at Mequon, just a few miles away, commuting from home.

But there it had happened. The unthinkable. In the early days of marriage, Norm had always joked to his friends, "Give your children wings, and let them fly." But he came to rue that glib remark.

For at Concordia Ruth had met and fallen in love with a young exchange student, Emanuel Martinez from Mexico City.

A *Mexican*! Norm couldn't believe it. Nor could he blot out the prejudice he had against Mexicans. There were few of them in lily-white Cedarburg. Oh, he remembered seeing some of the greasers (his dad called them that) standing outside a filthy bar on the edge of town. But they were lower-class people. *Mexicans*! And my own daughter, Ruth, falling in love with one!

Ruth said, "But you know *nothing* about Emanuel and his people—their strong, loving families, their constant hard work ... and yet their joy ..."

And Norm would withdraw. And at times he would

42

think, *God forgive me for my prejudice. You love all people as much as you love me. Forgive me, Lord.*

But Norm still couldn't get over it.

Well, Norm rationalized, at least Emanuel was a cut above his people. *Or was that a racist thought also?* Besides his fluent English—Emanuel spoke with only a bare trace of an accent—Emanuel had also mastered French, and he worked hard. There was no doubt about his ability to support Ruth.

And he did feel sorry for the guy. His whole family had been wiped out in an earthquake in Mexico City—father, mother, and six brothers and sisters. Only his grandmother remained alive, refusing to leave her home west of Mexico City in Toluca. She was well cared for by old friends.

Well, Norm hoped the romance would pass, but it didn't. Norm watched them graduate together at Concordia University and then, since Emanuel couldn't get a job of any kind in the states, he returned to Mexico City for a translator's job at one of the embassies. And then—well, it all took place too fast for Norm. Ruth went down to see Emanuel— "just for a visit." Norm tried to talk her out of it, fearing the worst. But it happened. She returned, engaged. Emanuel had taken instruction and joined the church. And soon afterwards Ruth and Emanuel were married at their church in Cedarburg.

Norm sighed. My only daughter marrying a Mexican! How could she do it? Rejecting her own culture, her people, her home. Again Emanuel tried to find work in the Milwaukee area but to no avail. So the day came when Norm saw them off at the plane in Milwaukee. And he came home to their empty house on Pine Street and sat down in his old easy chair in the front room and cried.

"I'll be home several times a year, Dad. You'll see," promised Ruth. "I haven't left you forever. I love Emanuel. I'm his wife now. I must go where he goes ... be with him. He's my *husband*, Dad." And she too had cried.

Then came *the visit*. Ruth and Emanuel had settled into an apartment in a suburb of Mexico City, and Ruth pleaded with Norm to come stay with them for a while. So Norm made the trip. But what he experienced revolted him even more.

Mexico City—and the little cubicle they lived in on the

outskirts of town. Norm just couldn't see his daughter living this way the rest of her life!

The apartment was only three tight little rooms. On the ninth floor of a large complex, their one living room looked out over a courtyard and the busy street below. Norm resented the setting from the beginning. People living in their tight little boxes with tiny balconies and aluminum railings looking like bars on a small cell. The jail in which they would spend years of their lives. It would be to work each day and then back to the small box each night and then one day they would all die and someone would put them in another small box in the earth.

And Ruth and Emanuel would never be able to afford a home. And Norm's modest pension money couldn't help them—as if *he* would ever ensure their staying in Mexico by helping them buy a house!

After Norm's arrival, he tried to brighten the place up a little. He couldn't have his little Ruth living this way. So he bought some planter boxes (which they couldn't afford) and put them on the balcony. And one day Ruth came home from work and saw the colorful profusion of potted plants and trailing geraniums cascading down from her little balcony, and Ruth sat down and cried. But the next morning after she left for work Norm went out on the balcony alone, lit up a cigar and sat down. A few neighbors were hanging out their wash on racks on their little balconies. Others, in their pajamas, stood silently staring at him, cigarettes in their hands, or leaning over their railings gazing impassively at the street below.

It was all too much for Norm. He had another whole day ahead of him, waiting for Ruth to return. His little Ruth. How could this have happened to her?—to *him*?

She had left her home, her culture, all the things she had known. All gone, behind her, forgotten, for the love of Emanuel. And for a life like *this*!

Norm looked inside the living room. There was their mangy cat, Alfredo, on top of their old battered piano, snaking its way between pictures and bric-a-brac, not disturbing one item. It drank its water from a leaky faucet in the bathroom. Sometimes it nimbly walked the railing of the balcony. Norm hoped it would fall off.

Across the street far below, Norm watched the same scene every morning. At precisely 8 a.m., a man emerged from a garage door pulling a cart after him. He was bearded and stood erect. A pipe dangled from his mouth. He crossed the street, went through another garage door, and closed it. Norm would not see him again until late afternoon.

The sights and sounds of the panorama below continued to assail him. Most noticeable of all was the pervasive scent from the *comales*, the little grills where the *masa* was being cooked.

Then there were always small motorbikes whizzing by, constantly accelerating, buzzing like hornets or pesky horse flies. Occasionally one would stop at the ratty-looking sidewalk cafe on the other side of the street. The rider would ease off his bike, jerk off his helmet, spit, light up a cigarette, engage in small talk with the patrons for a while, and then spin off in a seemingly pointless direction.

Several blocks away, on eye-level with the balcony where Norm sat, was an old church. Its out-of-tune bell rang every quarter hour. Gilt-painted, modern hands on the clock were always two minutes ahead of the hour.

Down below, another broken alarm went off in a car. Whooeee! Whooeee! Whooeee! It wailed for 15 minutes before someone disengaged it.

The grinding roar of the traffic never seemed to end. There were filthy buses (no emission controls required here), their exhausts belching out stinking, gaseous fumes. Dogs barked intermittently in the courtyard.

Next door, Ruth had told him, lived two young "*Maricones.*"

Yesterday they had had a fearful fight. One locked the other out on the balcony. There were screams and insults. The one smashed a window to get back into the apartment. There were more shouts, then silence for four hours.

Suddenly, across the courtyard far below, Norm heard screams. There, running from a large barking German Shepherd, was an unbelievably comic sight. A large, actually obese, middle-aged woman had just dropped two huge bags of groceries and started running. Her frizzy hair went in all directions. Her makeup was overdone, her mascara streaked, her breasts bouncing as her high heels clacked her some 60 feet away from the dog, where she stopped. A neighbor pulled the dog inside, and the woman returned to retrieve her scattered groceries, cursing and muttering all the while. Ruth said the neighbors said she was an ex-whore.

Now the whine of a car vacuum cleaner began again at the nearby filling station. That went on all day, too. And always the cars, buses, trucks, going by, accelerating, accelerating, accelerating. And the buzzing gnaaa! gnaaa! gnaaa! of the motor scooters, the riders leaning forward, direction unknown.

And the people on the sidewalk, rushing, rushing, rushing. He particularly hated going to the market with Ruth. People were always pushing him aside, chattering rudely away in a language he could not understand. *Those guys at the Tower of Babel really blew it!*

It was all too much for Norm. Cedarburg was never like this!

The whole vexing situation simply overwhelmed Norm. He flicked his dead cigar nine stories down to the dirty courtyard below, and went out to buy more cigars.

That night he confronted Ruth. Emanuel was not yet home.

"Ruth, baby," Norm began. "How can you live ... like *this*?"

"What do you mean, Dad?"

"Well, how could you leave the place God put you in—Wisconsin, your own culture, everything you grew up with? It just doesn't make sense."

"But, Dad," Ruth began, "the whole world is God's culture. God's world is not just Cedarburg, or Milwaukee, or even the whole USA!"

"*But ... this!*" Norm said agitatedly, pointing out to the noise-filled street below.

"But, Dad," Ruth said seriously, "I could show you the same kind of life in a barrio in LA, or a ghetto in Philadelphia or New York City, or even the back streets of Milwaukee. It's right in your own backyard, too. It's just that you never go there."

"But, Ruth," Norm began again, but the phone was ringing.

Feeling shut out, Norm listened as Ruth chattered away in perfect Spanish to some friend. Finally the phone call was over and Norm irritatedly asked, "And who was that?"

Quietly Ruth responded, "That was Maria. Remember you met her briefly the first night you were here?"

"Oh yes," said Norm, recalling the diminutive, sad-eyed factory worker who had clung to Ruth's side as they stood together down in the parking lot.

And then Ruth began to explain. "Maria is pregnant. Her boyfriend left her when he found out. I've talked her out of suicide twice. I'm the only real Christian friend she has. No family. She's alone in the world. I've shared the Gospel with her many times. In fact, she's going to be confirmed next Sunday. Don't you see, Daddy? I'm here because my place is with Emanuel. I'm his wife. I love you and always will. But if for no other reason, I believe God also wanted me here—just to help Maria. That's the way you and Mom brought me up, Dad. To share the Gospel."

Stunned, Norm replied, "But, Ruth, baby, you can be a missionary right back in Cedarburg!"

"But Daddy, my home is here now with Emanuel. Don't you *understand* that yet?" And she began to cry.

Norm sat in silence. *So I had to give up my only daughter so she could marry a man from a foreign culture and desert me and live in a strange land far from me and just so ONE person could hear the Gospel! It was all too weird.* Without realizing it he had spoken his thoughts aloud.

" ... and all just so this one person could hear the Gospel!"

Ruth was composed now. "Yes, Daddy," she said quietly. "Don't you remember Luke chapter fifteen? The *one* lost sheep. The *one* lost coin. That *one* person might be saved." Silence settled over them.

Norm sighed. So he had to give up his only daughter because God wanted her Christian witness for one person in a distant land. And then the pastor's words came back to him from the church in Cedarburg. "For God so loved the world that He gave His only begotten Son ..." *Only* Son!

They both heard Emanuel's key in the door and with a

mutual look ended the conversation as he burst through the door and hugged Ruth.

Dinner was prepared and eaten. Afterwards, they sat in the tiny living room and watched a soccer game on the small TV. At a break in the game Emanuel left the room for a moment. The phone rang. Ruth answered it, and as she did Norm noticed her face turn white.

"Emanuel!" she cried. Then she quickly whispered to Norm, "His grandmother just died!"

Emanuel entered the room and sitting next to Ruth picked up the phone. Ruth put her arms around him as he began, "Si?"

Norm gave a questioning glance in Ruth's direction. The look on her face and her nod toward the kitchen shot through Norm's heart like a bullet. She wanted him to leave the room!

And so he did. Getting up painfully he walked past the huddled couple, feeling crushed, absolutely crushed. He was being directed out of his daughter's room, out of her home, out of her marriage, out of the depth of the long relationship he had had with his little Ruth. Norm Anderson: NOT WANTED!

It was the longest walk he ever took in his life.

Norm went into the kitchen and turned on the noisy water faucet so they couldn't hear him, and began to sob.

Not long afterwards Ruth came into the kitchen. She was shocked when Norm said, "You didn't want me *in* there, *did* you!?"

Wide-eyed, Ruth responded, "Dad, I can't *believe* you're upset. It had *nothing* to do with *you*. It was simply a moment we two had to be alone ..."

And then she went on to say that she simply hadn't wanted Emanuel's grief displayed in front of Norm. His grandmother had died, his last living relative, she explained again. And she didn't know how he would take it. But he had been calm. And they had sat in silence for a few moments after the call. And then Emanuel had said, "Now she is with the Lord—and the rest of the family." And that was it. They would have a simple memorial service in two days. And she would be buried there in the little village cemetery where her parents lay.

Norm stayed a few more days and went with them to the funeral. And then, out of words and out of pleas, he resigned himself and planned his flight home.

Ruth said, "I'll see you in just two months, Dad! It won't be long! See you in Cedarburg!"

Norm could not sleep on the flight to Milwaukee. Exhausted, he got into his car in the parking lot and headed for Cedarburg. Once or twice he dozed at the wheel but pulled himself awake just before heading off the road. Finally he turned down Pine Street. Just a few blocks and he would be home. Norm's eyelids blinked sleepily and his head nodded towards the wheel. A telephone pole loomed up in front of the headlights ....

"Norm!" Sandra was speaking to him again. "As I was saying, Maria was Ruth's close friend. Later, Maria died in childbirth. But she died a Christian—thanks to Ruth."

"Yes, Ruth brought me to Christ also," said Emanuel. And suddenly there *he* was, standing with Ruth at their side.

"But how?" Norm began. "Both of you here *already*? I thought you were still on earth."

Ruth smiled at her father. "Our children are still on earth, Dad. We were there for 50 years with them. It has not really been so long since we saw you last, has it, Dad?"

"But how," Norm began.

"There is no time in heaven, *Señor*," said Emanuel with a wink.

"Of course," said Norm, as the truth sank in.

"The Lord meant it all unto good," said Sandra.

"He does all things well, doesn't He?" said Ruth.

"Of course," said Norm.

For Discussion

1. How do you evaluate the decisions that Ruth made about her life? Was she wrong in leaving her widowed father? See Genesis 2:24; Ruth 1:16–17. Do you feel these Scripture passages are justification for the choices Ruth made?

2. What do you think of Ruth's reasoning that God wanted her in Mexico "if only for the sake of Maria"? (Scan Luke 15.)

3. Do you feel Norm was *basically* a prejudiced person? What led to any of his racist feelings? Do you think he was trying to overcome them?

4. What does Scripture say about interracial or cross-cultural marriages? See Galatians 3:28.

5. What are some of the *subtle* ways that racism and prejudice are evidenced in our lives?—in our congregations' approaches to our mission and ministry?

6. What are the *origins* of racist thinking? (Consider Galatians 5:19–21.) Mention *specific* ways in which it can be confronted in the home and the church.

7. Your congregation is totally European American in its membership. For the first time, an African American family of five visits your worship service. What do you think the reaction would be? What would *you* do?

SESSION 5
Death/Life

Sentimental Journey

Pastor Walter J. Lamb drove toward the Maryknoll Retreat Center near Baltimore. On his way to a pastoral conference on preaching, he pondered his involvement. At 70 he wouldn't be preaching much anymore. Retirement faced him. His wife had died a year ago—it seemed like yesterday. The ache of losing her still grieved him. His children were in distant cities.

Why the conference? He didn't need more lectures. But he did need the fellowship of the pastors. He felt lonelier than he had ever been.

Not many years ago he hadn't felt this way. But now he felt differently about living and dying. Young people, even middle-agers, just *don't understand.*

What purpose is there in life, with death all around him? He looked at the flowers beginning to bloom beside the freeway. They lived now but soon they would die.

He recalled last Monday's visit to the Vietnam Memorial in Washington, D.C. He had approached the long black marble slab with its countless names. As he walked along, his attention focused on a name with a red heart pasted on it.

Below it lay a huge, beautiful spray of flowers, and beside it, a three-page letter, under clear plastic, which a mother had written to her dead son. People were kneeling to read it, and he did, too.

"Dear Son," it began, "I come here again to place my heart on your name. It was on my birthday, 25 years ago today, that you were killed in Vietnam ..." He read on, the mother recapping her son's story. She told how she heard that other soldiers had turned into animals in combat, but her son had not. Somehow he had managed to keep the same happy-go-lucky attitude he'd had as a boy. The mother ended with the words (Walter copied them on a scrap of paper): "And so I come again on this day, my birthday, and the day of your death, to place my heart upon your name. But this I know—I would rather have had you for 21 years and all the pain that goes with losing you, than never to have had you at all. Mom."

When Walter had finished scribbling his note, he heard a voice: "Did you like my letter?" Looking up, he saw a neatly dressed woman—perhaps in her middle 70s—standing beside him.

Walter mumbled something about how helpful her letter was. Then she introduced her husband. He stood nearby on crutches, a war ribbon on his lapel. They talked for a few moments, and then the woman said, "And you know, 10 years ago, I told my daughter, 'If you ever have a child, I'll never cry on this day, my birthday, the day of my son's death—*ever again!*' You know," she added, "5 years ago today, she gave birth to a son—on this *very day*."

People pushed around the three of them, trying to read the letter. Walter managed a few more words of thanks to her, and walked away. He was struck by the perspective that mother had!

In parting, he walked past the Lincoln Monument, and had seen a 6'4" Marine, ramrod-straight, walking ahead of him with his girlfriend.

He had overheard the Marine—with his crewcut and banjo ears—speak excitedly about his transfer from Quantico to El Toro Marine Base in Southern California.

57,000 dead in Vietnam, Walter mused. And 75,000 Vietnam vets had attempted suicide. Now another young man being prepared for war. He wondered how many ways they had trained *him* to kill another man.

Death. And still more death.

When he arrived at the retreat house, Pastor Lamb

pulled himself from his reverie, quickly registered, and began a tour of the massive complex—a combination conference center and retirement home for nuns, including a beautiful chapel on spacious grounds. With the aid of the nun who served as a tour guide, Pastor Lamb continued his tour. Turning a corner, he noted a door ajar and glanced into a nearby room. To his surprise, the room contained a corpse in a casket, with nuns kneeling, telling their beads. The nun quietly remarked, "Sister Agatha died yesterday." "Sister Lucy, upstairs, is 93," she continued. "She finished reading *The Shroud of Turin* today."

As he passed another room he saw 20 other nuns, prayer books open, chanting, telling their beads.

All waiting to die, he thought bitterly. Am I next?

When he asked for a key to his room, he was told, "There is no key. The door is unlocked; but you can lock it from the inside, if you wish."

What did that mean? "I think there's a sermon illustration there," he mused, his mind quickening.

Walter found the conference satisfying. He enjoyed being with other pastors, sharing the same agonies and joys, but also sharing frustrations and occasional glimpses of hope for their wandering sheep. (How did Jesus ever put up with *His* dumb disciples!? He must always have been saying "UFDA!")

One pastor arrived late because he had a funeral. Another one recounted how, in his small town's garbage dump, they had just found the dismembered bodies of two people, well-known in the community. More death.

He heard another talk about the high school teacher in his parish who asked her students what they thought they would be doing in 25 years. Not a one could answer. Why? They didn't think they would be alive. Drive-by shootings. Gangs. Guns. DEATH. That was their fear.

So what did they do? *Float.* Take drugs. Or go to college, graduate with a B.S., and find there are no jobs. Back to college and get an M.A.—and then, if ...

Another pastor interrupting, quickly finished the sentence, "And then engineering, ending up over-qualified and unable to get a job that will care for the family. Suicide seems the only way out. It *happened* in my parish. Man 34 years old. Plastic bag over his head."

Death, pondered Pastor Walter J. Lamb. Who's kidding whom?

One afternoon during a break in the conference, Walter left the retreat center to drive downtown to get gas for his car. On the freeway he had to swerve quickly to escape disaster. No time to brake! Dear God! A heavy tow-truck, with a car in tow, had rear-ended a slow-moving car some distance ahead of him. He jerked to the left lane just in time, and then looked back, assessing the scene. No overturned cars, just a mess. Traffic honked behind him. He *moved*.

His could have been the car the tow-truck hit. Horrible accident. Many killed. *Death.*

But he had swerved in time. Surely. Adeptly. Why am I so obsessed? *Do I really want to die or to live? Am I more afraid of life than death?*

The convolution of ideas began to muddle his mind.

When he returned to the retreat center, Walter heard the automatic tolling of a bell over the intercom. Somber, every five seconds or so. A fire alarm? He asked a sister. "Oh, no. They're taking Sister Agatha out for burial now."

The bell droned on—filling the huge building with its ominous tone.

" 'The bell tolls for *you*,' Walter J. Lamb," he sighed.

But as he opened the door to his room, his mind turned to some words of the apostle Paul to the Philippians.

> I am caught from both sides: I want very much to leave this life and be with Christ, which is a far better thing; but it is much more important, for your sake, that I remain alive. I am sure of this, and so I know that I will stay. I will stay on with you all, to add to your progress and joy in the faith. So when I am with you again you will have even more reason to be proud of me, in your life in Christ Jesus.

Walter stepped to the window of his celllike room in the Maryknoll Retreat Center—in Maryland—USA—the World—God.

He saw flowers. Blossoms. Hobbling across the parking lot was an old nun, smiling, assisted by a young nun with her order's cap. But it looked like she was almost wearing shorts.

I'm too old for that, he chided himself.

"You know, Walter," his side-kick pastor-friend Ben had said, "It's always our hearing that goes second."

"Arghhh!" he groaned, pulling himself away from the window.

"I'm still mad at God. No," he quickly countered, penitent, "I'm mad at *you*, Death! I know you are going to come! Well, come on, then!"

Just before the two nuns, the very old one and the young one, disappeared into the nearby forest, Walter saw the younger nun evidently ask the older one for a blessing.

A tender scene! With her left hand, the older nun steadied herself with her cane. She blessed the half-kneeling younger nun on the forehead with the sign of the cross. Then they lightly embraced and walked off radiantly into the woods.

Walter blinked the tears out of his eyes—he was a sucker for old Shirley Temple movie endings, and he berated himself for (1) invading the privacy of the two nuns' sacred moment together, and (2) being just another dumb disciple.

For then he remembered the note of hope his young intern had sounded in his sermon the previous Sunday. The student had quoted a bad novel (worse movie, with Lana Turner), James Gould Cozzens' *By Love Possessed*. "In the midst of life, we are in death." The student was talking about the hopeless girl who committed suicide.

"But I say to you today," he'd concluded, "and this is not just 'the church's' faith, but *my* faith. In the midst of death, *we* are in *life*!

"And now in the Holy Eucharist we will celebrate that Great-Meal-to-Come in the heavenly banquet hall.

"In the midst of death *today* ... I *know* ... I say, we all are in *life* ... through our Baptism into Christ. Life eternal, through Jesus Christ, our Lord."

Still gazing out the window, the Reverend Walter J. Lamb, pastor for 45 years, suddenly didn't know how to pray.

But he remembered what his mother had said her mother had taught her: "If you fall asleep saying your prayers, don't worry. The Holy Spirit will finish them for you."

So he looked out at spring in Maryland, the new life, the blossoms, the greening grass, the tender buds and shoots of new hope and *thought*—and *hoped*—it was a prayer.

"Dear God, please be patient with me. You have been for so long. Show me the work You still want me to do. In Your Word, You have taught me how to die—trusting in You.

"Now—teach me—once more—how to *live*."

For Discussion

1. It's a *depressing* story, isn't it! Well, death *is* depressing. Or didn't you relate to it? Why or why not?

2. Is it self-pity or simply being human to have some remorseful thoughts about one's own eventual death?

3. What might Pastor Lamb's insight have been at the discovery that there was no key to his room—but it could be locked from the *inside*? Consider Hebrews 2:14–15.

4. We are all terminal! But often we act and live as if we will never die. How does Scripture help us to live "eschatologically"—sensitive to "the last times" of the world and our own lives? On watchfulness for Christ's return see Matthew 25:13; Luke 12:37; 1 Thessalonians 5:5–6; Revelation 3:11, 16:15. On watchfulness against sin and temptation see Matthew 26:41; Acts 20:31; 1 Corinthians 10:12, 16:13; Colossians 4:2; 1 Peter 5:8.

5. How does one find the balance between being "willing to live—but ready to die"? Can you agree with the apostle Paul's answer to that question? See Philippians 1:21–26.

6. Consider the following prayers. What do they say to you?

A Homesick Angel

Remind me daily that I am a stranger, pilgrim, and exile in this land, O Lord. Here I have no continuing city. My driver's license has the wrong address. My permanent residence is in heaven, from whence I look for Your return. Let me therefore live "as if there were a homesick angel within my heart," knowing there is no perfect place or security within this life.

And while my death may not be near, make me ever watchful for the imminent appearance of You, my Master. And grant that such days as I yet have during this sojourn be wisely used in preparation for return to my heavenly home—and Your blessed presence. In Jesus' name. Amen.

Watching for the Heavenly Pattern

Tho tangled threads on this side I see
Of the tapestry of life You are weaving for me
Give me a glance of what You see
What the finished pattern is going to be
All-wise Heavenly Father, please give me some of
    Your wisdom.
Give me the spectacles of Your Spirit that I may see
    the Heavenly Pattern:
Blessing
Dancing
Elation
Temptation

Grant me the sensitivity to know that "You observe (me) at the start of each day, and You put (me) to the test without warning" (Job 7:18).

While I am prancing about with joy over a victory, remind me to thank You first of all for an undeserved gift. Then move me not to become presumptuous for additional blessings at this moment.

Rather prepare me for the certain return of new testing. Humble me lest I become falsely self-confident. Order my mind to accept the cycle of grace followed by trial. Make me realize that Your Heavenly Pattern would not seem so strange to my puny mind if I knew *You* better.

Let me guard my demeanor that when my hope fades I may not despair, but wait patiently upon You, knowing Your heavenly consolation will return. For then I shall say with the psalmist: "You changed my sorrow into joy and wound me around with gladness" (Psalm 30:12). In Jesus' name. Amen. (See Psalm 30:7; 30:8; 30:9; 30:11.)

Ready to Die—Ready to Live

Lord, help us realize that we are all TERMINAL. We are dying persons. Each one of us is dying right now. It is only a matter of time before our own death. We may say, "But the insurance tables show I have so many years to live, and I am in good health." But beyond the fact that an accident or disease could rapidly change all that, help us to learn—as Scripture teaches us—to live as dying persons. For only one who is ready to die is really ready to live.

Give me Your heavenly insight that this is not a morbid thought but an exciting one. It means I will receive far more out of each day from You than I do now, for I will live each day more for itself. Grant me a detachment, therefore, and yet a certain zest and vividness at the same time, knowing I shall pass this way but once. "This day will never come again!" Therefore let me rejoice and be glad in it. I am an exile from my heavenly home. Let me therefore live like one! In Jesus' name. Amen.

SESSION 6
Testing/Trials

The Best Christmas Present I Ever Had

Young Pastor Mike Fisher headed his car toward the home of Carlos and Maria Hernandez on the outskirts of Albuquerque. He was still reeling and hurting from the tragic message in Carlos's phone call.

It was hard to believe. Six weeks ago Maria had given birth to twin girls, Rosita and Lucia. Because she had had tuberculosis in her native Guatemala before coming to the United States, the doctors had advised her to stay in bed for six weeks. So Carlos and Maria had not been in church during that time. Pastor Mike had been in their home often. But last night he and the prospective godparents had come by and they planned the Baptism of the twins for the following Sunday.

Then came Carlos's heartbreaking news on the phone just 20 minutes ago.

"Pastor," he sobbed in a broken voice, "Lucia died last night. We don't know how—or why. But when we looked in the crib this morning she was ... *cold*." Mike had spoken a few words of comfort to Carlos. But then, worried about Maria, he said he would be at their home as soon as he could.

SIDS again. Sudden Infant Death Syndrome. It would

probably be the same desolate, unsatisfying answer he'd gotten for parents before from the funeral home—after the pathologists finished their tests. No explanation. No one at fault. It just *happened*. And medical science had not yet been able to explain why.

Pastor Mike entered the small duplex and immediately put his arms around Maria. He just held her quietly for a few moments.

"Rosita is sleeping," is all Maria could say. Mike nodded silently and after a moment said, "Carlos, please get a bowl and put some warm water in it." He nodded and disappeared into the kitchen. Soon the little ceremony began. The table was cluttered with newspapers and laundered baby clothes. So Mike simply put the baptismal bowl on top of the TV set. Maria brought in Rosita and held her in her arms as Pastor Mike said a brief prayer. Then he continued:

"Rosita Carmelita Hernandez, I baptize you in the name of the Father, and of the Son, and of the Holy Ghost. Amen."

Mike stayed with the Hernandez's for several hours. He assured them that their child Lucia was in God's hands, in His loving care. He did not try to give heavy theological answers to their agonized whys. But he did remind them that God has lost His child, too, on the cross. *No.* Not "lost." God had *given* His Son to die for us.

And Lucia was not "lost." "Because we know where she is now, don't we?" he said firmly. "*In heaven,* 'with the Lord.' "

And then they planned the funeral. It was held the next day, in their meager home. Maria was too weak to go out. A few friends from church were there. The little white casket was placed by the living room window. Lucia lay still, as if only sleeping. In her hand was a tiny flower blossom. Pastor made the ceremony brief.

He read the Twenty-third Psalm. And then he rephrased it in his own words, applying it to them.

The Lord is my shepherd,
I shall not want;

He makes me lie down
in green pastures.
He leads me beside
still waters;
He restores my soul.

He leads me in paths
of righteousness
for His name's sake.

Even though I walk
through the valley of
the shadow of death,
I fear no evil;
for Thou art with me;
Thy rod and Thy staff,
they comfort me.

Thou preparest a table
before me
in the presence of
my enemies;
Thou anointest my head
with oil,
my cup overflows.

Surely goodness and mercy
shall follow me
all the days of my life;
and I shall dwell
in the house of the Lord
forever.

Having You, O Lord
I lack nothing.

One day I'll walk
in the New Jerusalem,
hand in hand
with my child!
Thank You, Lord. You
give me the strength
to begin each new day.

I praise You, Lord,
for forgiving all my
sins through the blood
of Jesus Christ, I bow
before His holy name.

You are with me!
I am not alone!

I see footsteps ahead
of me in the valley.
Lord, I know they
are Yours.

What a blessing to partake
of the cup
of Holy Communion,
united with the entire
body of Christ
and with my child.
I look forward to
sitting down together
one day at
the heavenly feast
to come!

Thank You
for Your strength
and mercy again this day,
Lord. I will love and
praise and serve You
forever!

Subsequently Pastor Mike visited Maria every day, for some weeks, but she could not be comforted.

"I blame my*self*, pastor. Oh, not for Lucia's death. But that she was not *baptized*. It's *my* fault. If I had not had the TB and had to stay in bed those weeks ..."

"But, Maria," Mike repeated, "Lucia was redeemed by God, loved by God, and from her conception was forever in His 'everlasting arms.' " He stressed the words of St. Augustine: "It is not the lack of Baptism, but the contempt of it that damns."

"The thief on the cross, to our knowledge, may neither have been circumcised nor baptized, and yet our Lord said to him, 'I tell you this: today you will be in Paradise with Me.' "

"Further," Mike continued, "in the Old Testament, God commanded that the male children *not* be circumcised *until* the eighth day. Would God reject a child who died before *that* day—the explicit day he had commanded? Certainly not. And how about all the female children—and the high mortality rate of infants in those days?"

"We leave these little ones to the grace and love of God 'Who does all things well.' "

As the weeks went by, however, Maria's doubts continued. One day Mike was at a pastors' conference in Tucson, and he mentioned Maria's ongoing grief to an older pastor.

Since his seminary days he'd always made a point of sitting at the feet of old veterans of the cross who had labored long and hard for the sake of the Gospel. He had discovered how nonlegalistic their views were. And when he, with his just-from-the-seminary fervency, found that people were not living up to his expectations, he learned from these old soldiers of the Kingdom some of the patience, the mercy, and the nonjudgmental ways they had evidenced in ministering to God's children—even as God has been immeasurably patient with us.

"Hmmm," mused old Pastor August Kleinschmidt. "You know? Why don't you check into the circumstances of the babies' birth at the hospital there in Albuquerque? Sometimes they baptize twins."

The minute he was back in town Mike drove straight to the hospital. He knew the head nurse in obstetrics, Mrs. Morales.

"The Carlos Hernandez twins?" she said. "Oh, I remember them well. The girls were both baptized. We *always* baptize twins."

Mike was elated. He left Mrs. Morales's office and in walking past the maternity ward remembered other times he had been in that nursery, masked and scrubbed, baptizing an infant in an incubator with a sterilized spoon of water from an immaculately boiled coffee mug.

Hurriedly he drove out to the Hernandez's home. It was now just two days before Christmas. The driveway was empty. Carlos was no doubt at work. He knocked firmly on the door. Maria appeared, Rosita in her arms.

"Good news, Maria! Lucia *was* baptized in the hospital. I just found out." And then he explained how. "Even without Baptism, she was still in God's love and care," he repeated. "But this should ease your own mind, Maria. Mrs. Morales, the head nurse in OB, assured me: *Lucia was baptized.*"

Then his eyes twinkled as he went on. "In fact, *Rosita* must have a special measure of grace since *she's* been baptized *twice!*"

Maria gave a forced little laugh, but her tears, tears of joy, took over.

"You know, Pastor Mike," she said after a moment, "this is the *best* Christmas present I *ever* had!"

They talked for awhile. But even after those relieving words, she still said softly before he left, "Pastor, they say 'time heals all wounds.' But, you know, it really doesn't."

As Mike drove home he knew he would be visiting Maria many more times. The news was "a Christmas present" all right. But contrary to what many people falsely thought, the grief period for Maria—and for Carlos—could last minimally for two years, even much longer.

Mike hit the sack early that night and in his prayers thanked God for the blessing of being a bearer of good news that day. At 4 a.m. he was awakened by the harsh jingling of his telephone.

"Pastor?" It was Carlos. "We're at the hospital. It's *Rosita!* Can you come right away? She's deathly sick, pastor. Our doctor's here, too, but we just don't know. *Can you come?*"

Mike said, "Of course," and in moments was in his car. He didn't want to even imagine the possibilities. Not *both* of the twins dead! As he drove, dumb cliche's drummed through his mind: "Why do bad things happen to good people?" "When it rains it pours." "Truth is stranger than fiction."

He turned on the radio. A cavernous-voiced cowboy singer was moaning: "What we need are faster horses, younger women, older bourbon, and more money."

"*I can't believe it!*" Mike groaned, as he flipped off the radio and ground into the hospital parking lot.

Soon he was with Carlos and Maria. He just held both their hands and looked directly into their eyes.

"Christ says, 'I will never leave you nor forsake you,' " he said simply.

"I know," said Carlos, as he and Maria slowly sank back on a waiting room sofa. Again they talked.

Carlos explained that they had checked Rosita at 2 a.m. and found she was breathing erratically. As her breathing became even more labored, they had called their physician and he urged them to rush the baby to the hospital where he would meet them.

She had been in an emergency room now for an hour.

This time Mike shared some of the psalms with them, especially the ones ending with the psalmist's joy at God's "coming through" after repeated affliction. Time dragged on.

"Just before you came, Pastor, Maria and I shared what our prayers had been as we rushed Rosita here to the hospital," said Carlos. "Maria said she was praying that God would spare Rosita's life. I was praying that God would give us the strength to bear up under whatever happened. Pastor, which prayer was ..."

The door of the waiting room burst open and a smiling doctor greeted the trio.

"Your child will be *all right*," he said, coming directly to the point. He beamed. "It's good you got her in here fast. But *everything's under control*." He explained the medical diagnosis in some detail. Then he added, "But after monitoring her for 12 to 18 hours, I think we may be able to let her go home later today."

"Thank God!" said Carlos.

"God be praised!" said Maria, making the sign of the cross.

Pastor Mike glanced at the date on his wristwatch.

"A Blessed Christmas Eve!" he exclaimed.

For Discussion

1. How do you feel Pastor Mike Fisher related to the Hernandez's problems? Why?

2. Was the pastor correct in baptizing Rosita so soon after reaching the Hernandez's home? Why or why not? What does Scripture say about the Baptism of children? See Matthew 28:19; Mark 10:14; John 3:5–6; and Acts 2:38–39.

3. Was Maria correct in "blaming herself" for Lucia's not being baptized? Explain.

4. St. Augustine said: "It is not the lack of Baptism, but the contempt of it that damns." Do you feel that lessens the necessity to baptize a child soon after birth? See Mark 16:16; Acts 22:16.

5. What factors are valid in delaying an infant's Baptism?

6. Under what circumstances should a lay person baptize a child?

7. In what situation should a person be rebaptized? Which was Rosita's "real" Baptism?

8. Which psalms end with God's always "coming through"— even though we suffer many afflictions? See Psalm 3; 6:9; 10:1 and 17; 16; 17:15—and many more.

9. Why does God permit affliction? See Hebrews 12:5–13.

10. Whose prayer on the way to the hospital was more appropriate—Carlos's or Maria's? Why? See Genesis 32:26; Matthew 26:39.

11. What Scripture passages promise that God will never test us beyond our strength to endure the trial? See 1 Corinthians 10:13 (afterwards, read verse 12).

12. *Which* gift from God was "The Best Christmas Present (Maria) Ever Had"?—the knowledge Lucia had been baptized, or the blessing that Rosita's life had been spared? Why?

HELPS FOR THE LEADER
Introduction

Please read "About This Book" at the beginning of this Study Guide. It is noted there that these short story Bible studies can be utilized in several ways:

❑ In small home-discussion groups
❑ In the Sunday morning Bible class
❑ In a weekday Bible class at church
❑ In individual reading and meditation for spiritual nourishment

There are 4, 6-session courses in this series. Each session is based on one to three short stories, arranged topically according to thematic issues, with discussion questions referencing Bible texts designed to lead the learner to apply Scripture to his/her own life.

Because the story/stories can be read in an average of 9 minutes (range, 5–13 minutes), the stories can be read at the time of meeting—either silently by each participant before discussion or aloud by selected readers in the group. A third alternative is that the stories be read beforehand.

Setting Up the Course

Whatever setting for a group is chosen, a key element in publicity is *This is a different kind of Bible study!* For example:

> *Jesus told stories.* And we are also going to deal with real-life stories from our world. In them we may see ourselves, seek to better understand ourselves, and see how we as Christians relate to other people. But our ultimate objective is reading "short stories leading into the Word." There, in "searching the Scriptures" we really determine who we are and whose we are and where we are going.

Beginning the Class
Size of the Group

Depending on how many people sign up to attend the course, decide how many separate groups you should have!

Remember, *the magic number is 10* (give or take 1 or 2). In groups larger than 10, many individuals don't have a chance to contribute. In too small a group some persons may feel intimidated and "freeze," especially on sensitive issues. If your class size is greater than 10, and you have only one leader, consider breaking into groups of four for small-group discussion of the questions (30 minutes). Then use the rest of the session for sharing with the total group the discoveries and the "help us with the answer to number ____" questions of the small groups.

Decide well in advance how many groups—and *prepared* group leaders—you should have.

The Setting

Be sure the group meets in as comfortable a setting as possible. Are participants more at ease around a table? Check the thermostat. Make sure the lighting is good.

Have refreshments arranged well ahead of time.

Provide extra Bibles and hymnals for those who don't bring their own.

Presession

As a group leader, be sure you arrive *before anyone else does*.

Welcome the arrivals. Introduce people who don't know each other. Don't presume they all do.

As participants are seated, be sure they can see each other.

Opening the Session

Begin with a brief prayer. Ask for the blessing of the Holy Spirit.

Then comment on the procedure:

- The story (stories) will be read (silently, or by a *good*, carefully selected reader).

- The discussion questions will follow.
- No one will be *pressed* to answer questions. No one will be embarrassed or "put on the spot."
- Turn to the *four key questions* in this guide and note how these are to be kept in mind in dealing with each story throughout the course:

   1. Is the story true to life? Give reasons for your answer.
   2. What, if anything, does the story have to say to our Christian faith and life?
   3. How does it reveal or point to our need? (Law)
   4. How does it point to or suggest God's action for us in Christ? (Gospel)

If some finish reading the story/stories before others, request that they reflect on the four questions until the others are done.

Note. In many groups, processing these four questions will consume *all* the time in a 50-minute session. Also, the questions after the story will probably take more than the time available. Therefore, decide on one of two strategies: *Either* agree to stick to the 1 or 1½ hour regular session time for each session, selecting among the questions only those that can be handled during the time available, *or* move through the stories and questions according to the interests of the group, leaving open-ended the amount of time it will take to complete the course.

The Art of Asking Questions

And now to some general considerations about your leading the discussions after the stories are read:

"Telling is not teaching." Learning does not occur as much when a discussion leader does most of the talking.

A good leader, therefore, utilizes the art of *inductive* questioning—"drawing people out."

Good questions facilitate INTERACTION,
- which yields INNER ACTION,
- which precedes LEARNING.

Good questions MOTIVATE learners to
- THINK and
- EXPRESS themselves and become more

INVOLVED in the process of their own
LEARNING.

What kinds of questions should you put to your group?
How to Teach Adults (St. Louis: CPH, 1992) recommends
questions that are
- **brief**—in as few words as possible.
- **open**—encouraging participants to think for themselves.
- **specific**—identified with words or ideas in your class
  Study Guide or used in your class conversations.
- **clean**—easily understood.
- **focused**—involving only one point.
- **purposeful**—stimulating the participant to
  —recall a fact or event;
  —analyze concepts and ideas and their relationships in
  order to discover meaning in them;
  —evaluate meanings to determine whether the participants agree or disagree with them and decide for or
  against them.
- **concrete**—calling for definite examples.

Don't answer your own questions. Wait for an answer—
even though the waiting period can seem interminable.

Avoid these types of questions:
- How could you even think about voting for such a liberal
  candidate? (Too harassing.)
- Tell us about the creation of the world. (Too vague.)
- Why must we support a candidate with views like hers?
  (Too leading.)
- What about a historical Adam and Eve? (Well, what about
  them?)
- Did Adam and Eve know what would result from their dis-
  obedience? (Too simple. Yes or no.)
- Did God create life anywhere other than on earth? (Too
  much speculation.)
- Come on now, you surely know the name of the first mur-
  derer, don't you? (Too condescending.)

For practice in formulating and evaluating questions,
evaluate the discussion questions in this book or in other
adult-education materials. What good questions do you see?
Why are they good or appropriate or helpful? How could
they be improved?

Undoubtedly, members of your group will raise some excellent questions. Be slow to answer them. Rather, bounce the questions back to the others in your group. That will help keep your discussions lively and interesting. Especially encourage people to use the words *why* and *how* as they begin their questions. Those questions lead to deeper thought and more precise application.

If you have one of the first two courses in this series— *The Perfect Couple* and *The Bright Red Sports Car*—see the introduction to the Leaders Guides for additional suggestions regarding the art of asking questions.

The Real Word for the Real World

A final point needs emphasis. Evangelical writer Elizabeth Elliott has said that "almost everything in the Bible is the reverse of what the world says." Certain group members, especially those addicted to some television talk shows, may have had their values shaped far more by the mass media than by the means of grace. As J. B. Phillips translates Romans 12:2:

> Don't let the world around you squeeze you into its own mould, but let God re-make you so that your whole attitude of mind is changed. Thus you will prove in practice that the will of God's good, acceptable to Him and perfect.

That kind of perspective comes only from our Lord Jesus Christ—cradled in the Scriptures. The Word interprets the world. It's not the other way around. Your task is to direct group members back to the values and priorities in God's Holy Word.

Toward that end, keep the four key questions of this series in mind.

1. Is the story true to life? Give reasons for your answer.
2. What, if anything, does the story have to say to our Christian faith and life?
3. How does it reveal or point to our need? (Law)
4. How does it point to or suggest God's action for us in Christ? (Gospel)

And may you be a prayerful, prepared, and compassionate discussion leader!

For additional help in your preparation, see *How to Teach Adults* (mentioned earlier) or "Developing Skills for Teaching Adults" from the *Teaching the Faith* video series (St. Louis: CPH 1993).

SESSION 1
Morality

Story

. The Secret Admirer

For Discussion

1. Could an incident like this have really taken place?

It certainly has! The question is how the pastor *handled* the situation (as is discussed in question 5).

2. Do you feel Frieda is responsible for her feelings, or was she "led on" by the pastor?

3. What do you feel really made Frieda pursue this course of action with the pastor?

Questions 2 and 3 are closely related. The pastor may not be as sensitive as he should be in projecting a "ladies' man" image. But Frieda is quite responsible for her own "magnificent obsession."

4. If you were Frieda's friend, what would you say to her and how would you help her? (Consider 1 Corinthians 10:13.)

This of course depends on how much Frieda reveals about the incident. But she certainly should be urged to work on her own marriage—and be more aware of Satan's battle plan against her. See 1 Corinthians 10:13.

5. How do you evaluate the pastor's approach in responding to Frieda? Is he guilty of a "misuse of power"?

Many group members may well feel he *is* guilty. At the same time he defused a potentially explosive situation.

6. Satan takes particular pleasure in attacking the moral stability of pastors. In your experience, when pastors "fall," has it more often been their fault or that of their temptress? or tempter!?

7. What are the scriptural criteria for a pastor's moral life? See 1 Timothy 3:1–7, 4:1; Titus 1:5–9.

8. Is it all right for a married person to "bond" with a person of the opposite sex if only for the purposes of a deep, enriching friendship?

Who's kidding whom? Satan is always alert, watching for such opportunities to implement improper intimacy, then lust, then fornication.

9. How does one avoid "magnificent obsessions" like Frieda's? See Matthew 4:10–11; 1 Corinthians 10:12–13; Philippians 4:8.

Story

No Thanks for the Memory

For Discussion

1. Need Yvonne have "confessed" to her husband? Would you have done so? Does one have to reveal everything from one's past to have a truly honest marital relationship?

This is a tough one. There may well be some things from the past that in all honesty one's spouse ought to know.

On the other hand, God's forgiveness is complete (See Isaiah 43:25). And as we are accepted "as we are," by Him, we are called to unconditional acceptance of each other.

2. If your mate had made a similar confession to you, how would you have reacted to it?

This question is not so much a request for an opinion, but a call to *live out* the Bible passage which says: "If you do not forgive men their sins, your Father will not forgive your sins" (Matthew 6:15).

3. To avoid hypocrisy, how much should we share with our friends about our weaknesses and sins?

It is not hypocrisy *not* to reveal all our sins. God knows us for what we are.

4. Aren't some sins practically "unforgivable"? If we can't avoid *remembering* a grave offense committed against us, how can we truly "forgive" it?

5. "Maybe God can 'forgive and forget' but humans can't." Do you agree? See Isaiah 43:25; Matthew 6:12; 14–15.

Questions 4 and 5 are closely related. *All* sins are forgivable. That's why Christ died on the cross for us.

That, of course, doesn't mean that we "sin more that grace may abound" (See Romans 6:1 RSV).

And although, humanly speaking, we "remember," we *can forgive*—or God is a liar. See 1 Corinthians 10:13; Philippians 2:13.

6. What is the nature of God's forgiveness? See Psalm 103:11–12; Luke 23:34; Romans 3:23–26.

It's abounding and full; complete and sure; based on the forgiveness won for us by Christ on the cross. God does not *excuse* sin. To do so, He would not be a just and holy God. Out of love for all of us who deserve punishment for our sins, God sent His Son to endure the punishment we deserve so that we might receive full forgiveness.

7. How often should one forgive? See Matthew 18:21–35; Colossians 3:13.

We receive *power* to forgive as we remember and live out the forgiveness we've received.

The Story

The Night Visitor

For Discussion

1. What would you have done if you had been in Ed's situation?

2. How do you evaluate Ed's feelings about Harold? Were they justified? How do you react to Ed's response at the end of the story?

Not particularly kind, was he? See Romans 12:19: "Do not take revenge, my friends."

3. Do you share Ed's feelings about television programs? Where do you think he is coming from theologically?

Ed had a wisely cynical view of the false values the mass media not so subtly seek to impose on us.

Do you agree with the following statement?

Why Phil and Oprah make lousy confessors, according to Father Raymond Tierney, C.S.C., in the *Vermont Catholic Tribune*: "A talk show host has no desire to correct whatever his guests are suffering from; in fact, he wants to keep them in their distortions because that is where the entertainment value lies. Healthy people are not entertaining."

4. What is the *source* of temptation? See 1 Peter 5:8; Matthew 15:19; James 1:14–15; 1 John 2:15–16.

The texts point to the "gruesome threesome": the devil; our old sinful nature; and the corrupted world in which we live.

5. What is one of the easiest ways we can fall into temptation? See 1 Corinthians 10:12; 1 Peter 5:9.

Overconfidence can be a major reason why we fall prey to our tempters. *Anyone* can fall. Thomas à Kempis in *The Imitation of Christ* speaks insightfully of how Satan tempts us. We have just come through a crisis or temptation and feel the *blessing* of God. Then comes dancing and elation. But we often forget the next step in the sequence:

- Blessing
- Dancing
- Elation
- *Temptation!*

It is when we are "riding high" that Satan is ready with his next temptation—in a different guise.

6. What promises does God make to us in overcoming temptation? See 1 Corinthians 10:13; James 4:2b; Deuteronomy 33:25b, 27; Isaiah 41:10.

One woman interpreted 1 Corinthians 10:13 quite profoundly. "The Lord doesn't ever give you more than you can handle"—*by His grace*.

7. What is the best way to prepare oneself *before* a particular temptation comes? See 1 Peter 2:2; Romans 6:1–6; 1 Corinthians 11:26–28; Philippians 4:8–9.

To repeat, we often doubt God or continue in misery because *we simply aren't hooked up to His means of grace*! Reflecting on His Word of promise; remembering what happened in our Baptism; feeding on the Word of forgiveness in Holy Communion empower us to resist temptation.

Prayer

Lord, keep me ever mindful of the high cost of forgiveness—the death of Your Son, my Savior. But assure me also—each day—that this forgiveness is mine when I come to You in penitent faith, trusting in Your mercy. And set me free from the plaguing memory of guilt over past sin, knowing Your blessed promise that when You forgive, You forget. In the strong name of Jesus Christ. Amen.

Hymn

"Chief of Sinners Though I Be" or "I Lay My Sins on Jesus"

SESSION 2
Trust

Stories

Just the Two of Us
The Fatal Phone Call

For Discussion

1. Who do you think was *initially* responsible for the strain in Bill and Trish's marriage? Do you think that is a fair question?

Men and women may respond differently to this question and fix blame on one person more than the other. But we do read: "No hand reached out to touch the other."

2. When a couple's careers diverge, what are the warning signs indicating estrangement? Similarly, for married or single persons, what causes friendships to falter or break up?

Answers may include failure to spend time together, forgetting to say "I love you," not *taking the initiative* in eliminating misunderstandings, etc.

3. What *really* causes "the fire to go out" in the bedroom? (Consider Ephesians 4:26.)

See the items above concerning question 2. But another clue is in Ephesians 4:26, which J. B. Philips paraphrases quite pointedly: "Never go to bed angry—don't give the devil that sort of foothold."

4. In Trish's mind, what was the significance of the quick kiss and hug she gave the doctor's medical assistant?

In keeping with her characteristic exuberance, it was undoubtedly an expression of her innocent joy.

5. Do you believe Bill was justified in his initial reaction to what he saw under the eucalyptus tree?

"Humanly" speaking, yes. But he should have known his wife better—*and* Satan's subtle suggestions to his jealous mind.

6. What do you think of the following statement?

> **I don't believe jealousy is all that bad. The dictionary says it means "(1) suspicious; apprehensive of rivalry; as, her husband was *jealous* of the other man." It also means "protecting" or "watchful." What's wrong with that? I don't want to lose my wife to someone else.**
>
> **In fact, the other day, when I made a comment about my wife flirting with a guy, she said to me proudly, "Why, Frank! You're JEALOUS!" It made her feel good I was JEALOUS. And then she added teasingly, "I didn't know you *cared* for me that much!"**

Answers will vary.

7. In one sense, these two stories have a common theme. Of course, many other factors than inability to have a child threaten a marriage. The real issue at stake is *trust*. In a lecture, British evangelist Canon Bryan Green once spoke of how he first asked his wife to marry him. He asked her if she loved him. She responded negatively. Then he asked her if she *trusted* him. She replied affirmatively. "That'll be enough to get on with it!" he concluded happily. What does Scripture say about the right kind of (trusting) thoughts? See Romans 12:3; Philippians 4:8; Ephesians 4:31–32.

8. What is the first thing you look for as a man, as a woman, in a spouse? How do you prioritize the qualities you desire in a mate?

Kindness, trust, patience, etc., will far outweigh physical attractiveness here. What qualities do the mass media and ads on TV hold up as primary?

9. Whether you are single or married, what do you look for most in making a friend? See Proverbs 17:17a; Ecclesiastes 4:9–10; John 15:13.

A peaceful, noncontentious spirit; helpfulness; self-giving love.

Prayer

Lord, please be merciful and forgive me for the times I have hurt my partner. By Your Holy Spirit enable both of us to forgive each other and to live selflessly for each other. Create a fresh bond of peace and mutual helpfulness between us that we may, by Your Holy Spirit's power, do Your will—both where we live now and wherever You call us to serve. In the strong name of Jesus Christ. Amen.

Hymn

"Love Divine, All Love Excelling"

SESSION 3
Pride

Stories

The Best Sunday School Teacher in the Congregation
Just a Servant

For Discussion

1. In "The Best Sunday School Teacher" why do you think Bill resented George Davis so strongly? One factor in his animosity and hostility was Davis's being "different" in his personality. Why do we have such a hard time accepting people who are different than we are?

The initial question here also relates to our Lord's effect on people. He was Sheer Goodness, and like light coming into a dark dirty room, His presence revealed people for what they were. They hated Him for it. And they killed Him for it. Bill's reaction to George Davis is similar.

2. What does Scripture have to say about the "difference of gifts"? What are its implications for our life together in a congregation? See 1 Corinthians 12; Romans 12:3–21; 1 John 3:14–20.

They are intended for mutual enrichment of all the members of the body of Christ, to enable us in peace and joy to reach out to others with the message of God's love in Christ.

3. What did the boys mean by Mr. Davis being their *friend* as well as their teacher? Are there times

this "friend" relationship can get in the way of good teaching?

To the latter question, yes—if proper discipline is ignored for the sake of "friendliness." But "teacher as *friend*" intimates compassion and caring—like "the Friend of sinners"—our Lord Himself.

4. A daughter added a note to her dad, on a Father's Day card: "Thanks for talking *with* me ... always." What do you think she meant?

She meant her father didn't talk *at* her. They respected where each other was coming from (as father and daughter) and both engaged in "active listening."

5. In "Just a Servant" Mary Lou took "pride" in her work and enjoyed lecturing. Is there anything wrong with that kind of pride?

Of course not. But her "pride" exceeded those boundaries.

6. What were the "cracks in the armor" of Mary Lou? Where did she "fall short"?

Note the comments about how waitresses should "know their place," "you're here to serve me," etc.

7. What qualities did you see in the waitress?

Note her cheerfulness, her open honesty about her Christianity, her humble withdrawal as "just a waitress," etc.

8. What does Scripture say about servanthood? See Matthew 20:26–28; Luke 22:27; John 13:14; Philippians 2:7.

Wanting to help people rather than make oneself "great"; being like Christ in being willing to do even the humblest and most menial of tasks in order to serve one another.

9. What are the beginnings of pride in each one of us? How do we recognize it? See Luke 18:11; 1 Peter 5:5b–6; Revelation 3:17.

"Putting down" other people; overevaluating ourselves; not giving God the glory for all we have and are.

10. What are other ways in which pride asserts itself in our daily lives—in the church? at work? at home?

This is a broad question. Respondents may be inclined

to comment on how *other* people assert their pride. The question is how *each* of us is tempted to do so.

Prayer

Move me out of the prison of my own little world, Lord, to the arena of sacrifice, self-giving, and service to Your suffering children. Teach me how to live not for myself but for others. Empower me—by Your Holy Spirit— not just to *speak*, but to *act*. In the strong name of Jesus Christ. Amen.

Hymn

"Take My Life, O Lord, Renew"

SESSION 4
Parenting

Story

The Longest Walk He Ever Took

For Discussion

1. How do you evaluate the decisions that Ruth made about her life? Was she wrong in leaving her widowed father? See Genesis 2:24; Ruth 1:16–17. Do you feel these Scripture passages are justification for the choices Ruth made?

You may wish to share this vignette by the author.

On Releasing My Children
First they were babies
so dependent
Then "the little ones"
Then "the boys" or
"the girls"
Now they're adults
I still feel constrained
to instruct
to guide
to mold
yes at times to
control them
Lord give me
the balance

to love
but not to smother
to dialogue
but not to dictate
to listen
but not
that I might better
manipulate
to *trust*
knowing how much
you love them too
to *release* them
to you

(From *Prayers for People under Pressure* [Milwaukee, WI: Northwestern Publishing House, 1992], p. 73. Reprinted by permission.)

2. What do you think of Ruth's reasoning that God wanted her in Mexico "if only for the sake of Maria"? (Scan Luke 15.)

The Lord always has concern for the *individual*.

3. Do you feel Norm was *basically* a prejudiced person? What led to any of his racist feelings? Do you think he was trying to overcome them?

Our culture certainly contributes to our racist thinking. At the same time, we are responsible for our own thoughts and actions.

4. What does Scripture say about interracial or crosscultural marriages? See Galatians 3:28.

Nowhere in Scripture is interracial or crosscultural marriage forbidden.

5. What are some of the *subtle* ways that racism and prejudice are evidenced in our lives?—in our congregations' approaches to our mission and ministry?

6. What are the *origins* of racist thinking? (Consider Galatians 5:19–21.) Mention *specific* ways in which it can be confronted in the home and the church.

THE basic origin of racist thinking is our innate pride and self-centeredness, our "original" sinfulness, from which racism and all evil acts flow.

7. Your congregation is totally European American in its membership. For the first time, an African American family of five visits your worship service. What do you think the reaction would be? What would _you_ do?

[A complete Bible study on this subject is available from CPH: _The Word for a Change_.]

Prayer

Lord, please help me to recognize the true nature of my inner being, which is so often self-centered. Forgive me! Mold me! Renew me! Make me daily Your new creation that I may become the self-in-Christ You want me to be. In the strong name of Jesus Christ. Amen.

Hymn

"Oh, Blest the House"

Death/Life

Story

Sentimental Journey

For Discussion

1. It's a *depressing* story, isn't it! Well, death *is* depressing. Or didn't you relate to it? Why or why not?

This calls for opinions. Some people may not feel like discussing death on a bright and cheerful Sunday morning. You may suggest to the group to think of an elderly person who was/is not far from death but is/was cheerful and "prepared." What was the clue to that person's frame of mind?

2. Is it self-pity or simply being human to have some remorseful thoughts about one's own eventual death?

It is human to sorrow for those who will grieve after you are gone. But a balance between sorrow and acceptance of death is found in the letter in the story "The Perfect Couple" in *The Perfect Couple and Other Stories* (Concordia, 1993).

3. What might Pastor Lamb's insight have been at the discovery that there was no key to his room—but it could be locked from the *inside*? Consider Hebrews 2:14–15.

This is only conjecture. Some group members may find an allegory here: Christ has set us free from our bondage to sin, the devil, and the fear of death. We ARE free, but so often "lock ourselves up" and fail to act upon what God has made us to be in Christ.

4. We are all terminal! But often we act and live as if we will never die. How does Scripture help us to live "eschatologically"—sensitive to "the last times" of the world and our own lives? On watchfulness for Christ's return see Matthew 25:13; Luke 12:37; 1 Thessalonians 5:5–6; Revelation 3:11, 16:15. On watchfulness against sin and temptation see Matthew 26:41; Acts 20:31; 1 Corinthians 10:12, 16:13; Colossians 4:2, 1 Peter 5:8.

Allow a few moments for volunteers to look up all the texts, each looking up a different one. Then have the texts read aloud. Allow for comments and questions.

5. How does one find the balance between "willing to live—but ready to die"? Can you agree with the apostle Paul's answer to that question? See Philippians 1:21–26.

By the power of the Holy Spirit—through the means of grace—God *does* give us the power to affirm Paul's confession.

6. Consider the following prayers. What do they say to you?

You may wish to read the three prayers in the Study Guide aloud and ask the group which phrases mean most to them in learning how to be "willing to live—but ready to die."

Prayer

How wonderful to get to know You better, Lord! Now I am going back to Your Word and again rediscover and then act on Your promises and challenges to me. O blessed Lord, make me a daily receiver of Your Holy Spirit that I may do Your will in my own household and also out in the world— the world Your Son suffered and died for. Change me, Lord! Move me, Lord! Use me, Lord! I'm ready now, Lord! In the strong name of Jesus Christ! Amen.

Hymn

"I Know That My Redeemer Lives!"

Testing/Trials

Story

The Best Christmas Present I Ever Had

For Discussion

1. How do you feel Pastor Mike Fisher related to the Hernandez's problems? Why?

He had a truly pastoral heart and was there when they needed him.

2. Was the pastor correct in baptizing Rosita so soon after reaching the Hernandez's home? Why or why not? What does Scripture say about the Baptism of children? See Matthew 28:19; Mark 10:14; John 3:5–6; and Acts 2:38–39.

Yes, he was fulfilling Christ's command and immediately moving to alleviate anxieties. Children are to be baptized because they are included in the "all nations" of Jesus' great commission. Moreover, as sinners, also babies need what Baptism offers. The Holy Spirit works through Baptism, a means of grace, to work faith even in babies who receive forgiveness as a gift. Baptism (by God's Word and promise connected with the water), forgiveness, and the Holy Spirit cannot be separated in the Sacrament.

3. Was Maria correct in "blaming herself" for Lucia's not being baptized? Explain.

Of course not. But her human/motherly reaction is understandable.

4. St. Augustine said: "It is not the lack of Bap-

tism, but the contempt of it that damns." Do you feel that lessens the necessity to baptize a child soon after birth? See Mark 16:16; Acts 22:16.

It does not. There are times when Baptism may not have been possible. We don't know the spiritual history of the one thief on the cross. But he made a clear confession, and Christ assured him that He would see him that day in Paradise. See Luke 23:42–43.

5. What factors are valid in delaying an infant's Baptism?

Christ's command—and blessing—are clear. Why delay Baptism?

6. Under what circumstances should a lay person baptize a child?

A child may be near death and a parent may need to baptize. The certainty that water was used and that the child was baptized "in the name of the Father and of the Son and of the Holy Ghost" is later verified by a pastor.

7. In what situation should a person be rebaptized? Which was Rosita's "real" Baptism?

A valid Baptism is a valid Baptism. Martin Luther said, "Once baptized, always baptized." We leave the second question in the Lord's hands. Both Baptisms were done in keeping with Christ's command.

8. Which psalms end with God's always "coming through"—even though we suffer many afflictions? See Psalm 3; 6:9; 10:1 and 17; 16; 17:15—and many more.

Ask individuals to look up the texts and, as time permits, read each aloud. Allow time for comments and questions.

9. Why does God permit affliction? See Hebrews 12:5–13.

We don't masochistically desire suffering or pain, but God does work in lives of His people in their suffering to draw them closer to Him. See also 1 Peter 2:19ff. and 1 Peter 4:12ff.

10. Whose prayer on the way to the hospital was more appropriate—Carlos's or Maria's? Why? See Genesis 32:16; Matthew 26:39.

Both were appropriate. Actually, the prayers were complementary.

11. What Scripture passages promise that God will never test us beyond our strength to endure the trial? See 1 Corinthians 10:13 (afterwards, read verse 12).

The point always is this: are we regularly hooked up to God's means of grace—His Word and Sacraments?

12. *Which* gift from God was "The Best Christmas Present (Maria) Ever Had"?—the knowledge Lucia had been baptized, or the blessing that Rosita's life had been spared? Why?

In her mother's heart, she certainly was thankful for *all* of God's blessings.

Prayer

Give me the precious insight of recognizing Your hand in my times of testing, Lord. By Your grace, give me the power to withstand temptation and not to fall. And help me always to remember that the purpose of my trial is to realize my need to lean more fully on You, my strength and my shield. In the strong name of Jesus Christ. Amen.

Hymn

"Oh, That the Lord Would Guide My Ways"

ACKNOWLEDGMENTS

About This Book

J. Russell Hale was quoted by Donald L. Deffner in *The Compassionate Mind: Theological Dialog with the Educated* (St. Louis: Concordia Publishing House, 1990), pp. 37–38.

Session 3

"Just a Servant" originally appeared in *The Lutheran Witness* 113:4, (April 1994), copyright © 1994 Donald L. Deffner.

Session 5

The three prayers are from *Soul Searching: Prayers for Students* (Fort Wayne: Concordia Theological Seminary Press, 1992), pp. 17, 25–27. Copyright © by Donald L. Deffner.

Session 6

The adaptation of the Twenty-third Psalm is from *At the Death of a Child: Words of Comfort and Hope* by Donald L. Deffner (St. Louis: Concordia Publishing House, 1993) pp. 26–27. Copyright © 1993 by Concordia Publishing House. All rights reserved.

Also my thanks go to Christina Wolff, David Owren, Earl Gaulke and the Educational Development staff of Concordia Publishing House, and to Jessica Wilmarth for outstanding work at the computer.